Religious America, Secular Europe?
A Theme and Variations

PETER BERGER
Boston University, USA

GRACE DAVIE
University of Exeter, UK

EFFIE FOKAS
The London School of Economics and Political Science, UK

ASHGATE

Published by
Ashgate Publishing Limited
Wey Court East
Union Street
Farnham, Surrey
GU9 7PT
England

Ashgate Publishing Company
Suite 420
101 Cherry Street
Burlington, VT 05401-4405
USA

Ashgate website: http://www.ashgate.com

British Library Cataloguing in Publication Data
Berger, Peter L., 1929–
    Religious America, Secular Europe?: A Theme and Variations 1. Secularism – Europe 2. Secularism – United States 3. Europe – Religious life and customs 4. United States – Religious life and customs
    I. Title II. Davie, Grace III. Fokas, Effie
    211.6'094

Library of Congress Cataloging-in-Publication Data
Berger, Peter L., 1929–
Religious America, Secular Europe? A Theme and Variations Peter Berger, Grace Davie, and Effie Fokas.
    p. cm.
    ISBN 978-0-7546-5833-7 (hardcover : alk. paper) – ISBN 978-0-7546-6011-8 (pbk. : alk. paper)
    1. Secularism–Europe. 2. Secularism–United States. 3. Europe–Religion. 4. United States–Religion. I. Davie, Grace. II. Fokas, Effie. III. Title.

    BL2747.8.B47 2008
    306.6094–dc22

2008009056

978-0-7546-5833-7 (Hbk)
978-0-7546-6011-8 (Pbk)

Reprinted 2009

Mixed Sources
Product group from well-managed forests and other controlled sources
www.fsc.org Cert no. SA-COC-1565
© 1996 Forest Stewardship Council

Printed and bound in Great Britain by
MPG Books Ltd, Bodmin, Cornwall.

Contents

Acknowledgments

The impetus for this book came originally from the Eurosecularity Project of the Institute for Culture, Religion and World Affairs at Boston University. We are grateful to the Pew Charitable Trusts and the Bradley Foundation for having generously supported this exercise. We would also like to thank Danièle Hervieu-Léger (President of the Ecole des Hautes Etudes en Sciences Sociales, Paris), who chaired the early meetings of the Project. The views expressed in this book are, of course, the responsibility of the three co-authors.

Chapter 1

Introduction

Both the substance and the structure of this book are captured in its title: it is an account of the relative religiousness of America and secularity of Europe and has a theme and variations. The *theme* of Eurosecularity is announced in an opening essay (Chapter 2) which introduces the comparison with the United States. The *variations* (four of them) are developed in the more detailed analyses that follow, each of which elaborates a particular line of argument. Quite apart from its content, the book is distinctive in the sense that it has three starting points and three authors. The 'threes', however, are somewhat differently constituted. The following paragraphs explain these various factors. The starting points are outlined first, then the book's contents. Once the contents are in place, each author and his or her particular responsibilities will be introduced.

Religious America, Secular Europe? A Theme and Variations should be seen first as an output from a project on European Secularity held under the auspices of the Institute on Culture, Religion and World Affairs at Boston University.[1] This project supported three workshops, held in Berlin between 2001 and 2003, with the cooperation of the Protestant Academy in Berlin. Each of these meetings gathered a distinguished group of specialists from all parts of Europe and beyond. The aim of the project was to understand better the exceptional nature of Europe's religious life compared with the trends in religion that are discovered elsewhere in the world. The deliberations of these meetings have informed the pages that follow.

A second stimulus can be found in the ideas set out in Grace Davie's *Europe: The Exceptional Case. Parameters of Faith in the Modern World* (2002), to which this book is in some respects a sequel. *Europe: The Exceptional Case* examines the religious life of Europe from the outside, comparing this with five other examples of Christianity (the United States, Latin America, sub-Saharan Africa, South Korea, and the Philippines)— asking in each case why the European trajectory is so different from most parts of the modern world, even the Christian world, in its comparative secularity. The present volume represents both a broadening and deepening of this idea, developing the argument in thematic rather than geographical terms.

More precisely, it draws out the comparison between Europe and the United States,[2] asking how two economically advanced societies, or groups of societies, can be so different in terms of their religious dimensions. Here the point of departure lies in the article prepared by Peter Berger (2005) for *The National Interest*, which has become Chapter 2 of this volume.[3] The questions that it poses are timely—and becoming more so almost by the day—given the on-going discussion about the unity/disunity of the West that dominates much of the political debate. The religious factor is central to these discussions, and is increasingly acknowledged as such. The latter remark is significant in itself: the recognition of religion as a credible and independent variable in both public debate and in the analyses of social science cannot be taken for granted. Its recent restoration after a long absence forms a core idea in the chapters that follow.

The notion of Eurosecularity unites these three initiatives. It also reverses what might be termed the "classical" perspective—that which assumed that European links between modernization and secularization were the model for the "rest of the world." This assumption, that is, the idea of an *organic* link between modernization and secularization, has dominated sociological thinking for the past 150 years—effectively since the beginnings of the discipline. Since 1970, however, it has been increasingly questioned. In the last quarter of the twentieth century, the markedly different situation in the United States, the growth of Christianity in the southern hemisphere, the presence of Pentecostalism all over the developing world, the affirmation of Islam in global affairs, increasingly heated debates for and against proselytism, and so on have prompted scholars of many disciplines to rethink the secularization paradigm as it was inspired by the European case and to question the assumptions on which it was built.

The number of books on this topic grows steadily as scholars revise their views on secularization. Jenkins (2002) offers an excellent example: what Jenkins calls *The Next Christendom* will not be found in the northern hemisphere, but in the global south. Indeed even the relatively buoyant statistics of religion in the United States pale into insignificance compared with the exponential growth of Christianity in the developing world, a phenomenon which (following Jenkins) eclipses even the much talked about expansion of Islam in the late twentieth century.[4] Relatively few of these analyses, however, are concerned primarily with a better understanding of the European case and why it is markedly different from the rest of the world.[5] This question—seen through the prism of a detailed comparison with the United States—is the principal goal of this volume.

The task is highly topical: the nature and development of Europe is central to public discussion. With this in mind it is essential that we develop a proper and fully European awareness of the historical evolution of which modern Europe is the product. A European writing of this history will reveal both its unity compared with the rest of the world and its internal complexity, once the very different histories of the constituent nations are taken into account. Religion is integral to this process, though Europeans are frequently surprised to discover this. Hence the vehemence of the reactions whenever religion encroaches on the public sphere in Europe. The furore surrounding the possible mention of religion in the preamble to the much debated European Constitution is a case in point. The presence of Islam raises similar issues. Indeed in many respects Islam has become the crucial catalyst—one that provokes Europeans to rethink the place of religion within Europe as well as outside. Similar issues are raised by the question of Turkish accession to the European Union. All of these illustrations will be examined in detail in the pages that follow.

It is clear, finally, that a different religious *formation* (to use the French term) leads to different visions of the world, different ways of thinking, and different sensibilities towards a whole range of issues—economic, political, cultural, and philosophical as well as religious. Nowhere is this more evident than in the current misunderstandings between Europe and the United States. The essential point is easily summarized: Europeans think that there is altogether too much religion in the United States, which has a dangerous effect on policy; Americans in turn are taken aback by Europe's secularity. Our aim is to throw light on these exchanges, appreciating that their origins very frequently lie in the different nature of religion in either case—and in so doing to contribute not only to a better understanding of the European situation, but to a more constructive transatlantic dialogue.

Hence the structure of the book. It is, as we have already indicated, a theme and variations. Chapter 2 contains the theme, which itself is divided into two sections. The first articulates the very different patterns of religious life that exist in Europe and the United States, bearing in mind that there are similarities as well as differences. The second follows naturally: why do these differences exist? What are the reasons for the very different trajectories of religious life in two undeniably developed parts of the world? Seven possibilities emerge: differences in church–state relationships; questions of pluralism; different understandings of the Enlightenment; different types of intellectuals; variations in culture and how this is understood; institutional contrasts (how in concrete terms the Enlightenment and associated cultures are sustained); and differences in the ways that religious organizations relate to indices of social difference (notably class and ethnicity).

In the chapters that follow, these explanations are grouped into the four variations, each of which begins from the ideas set out in Chapter 2. Effectively, however, these become a set of independent essays, each of which acquires a life of its own, developing the core ideas in different ways—the argument that emerges does not always concur with the initial statement or explanation. The most substantial "disagreements" concern the role of education in the secularization of European societies and the future of religion on the continent as a whole. An internal dialogue begins to emerge.

Chapter 3, for example, examines the different arrangements of church and state in Europe and the United States, bearing in mind the considerable diversity within Europe as well as the trans-Atlantic contrasts. Careful attention is paid to the different "presence" of religion in either case: in Europe, the existence of a state church or its successor (still a quasi-monopoly in many cases); in the United States, a seemingly limitless number of denominations. Both are explained by a distinctive history which requires detailed examination. Within these histories, the territorial embedding of the European churches, together with their relationships to power, becomes a crucial theme, the more so given its absence in the United States. The implications of both models for the continuing vitality of religion in the present period follows from this; so too do the consequences of increasing religious diversity found on both sides of the Atlantic. At the same time the chapter poses a question: are the patterns of religion in Europe becoming more like those in the United States? And what might be the consequences if they do?

Chapter 4 concerns culture rather than structure. The different understandings of the Enlightenment form the core of the argument, which draws amongst other things on Himmelfarb's recent writing. More precisely, the chapter asks how the essentially French idea of "freedom from belief" mutated as it crossed the Atlantic into a "freedom to believe"—and what are the steps or stopping places along the way? One point becomes immediately clear: even in Europe there are marked variations in how the Enlightenment was understood and how the epistemological shift that the Enlightenment represented related to the dominant religious tradition. France and Britain, for example, offer sharply different illustrations. The second part of the chapter examines this point from a different perspective, looking in particular at secular elites and how they have reacted to the presence of religion, not least its recent reappearance in public discussion. The latter point is interesting: as religion reaffirms its influence in the modern world, there is a need to revisit the secular philosophies that underpin modern political thinking. The difference between high and low culture is central to this discussion.

Different versions of the Enlightenment and different reactions to the presence of religion do not exist in a vacuum. They are carried in a range of institutions, some of which are created for the task and some of which find themselves co-opted, willingly or not. Chapter 5 deals with these institutions. Contrasting understandings of the state provide an obvious point of departure, an institution which in itself is differently conceived in Europe and America. This point needs to be grasped for its own sake, quite apart from its relationship to religion in all its manifestations. State churches, for example, imply a particular—essentially European— perception of the state, without which they cannot exist. Equally important are the institutions responsible for both making and interpreting the law, a complex and continuing process which takes place differently in Europe and the United States. So far at least, there is no equivalent in Europe to the American Supreme Court, which merits very careful attention. So too do the individuals appointed to it.

Within these overarching frameworks, education emerges as a very significant conduit for religious ideas—sometimes as a carrier of the dominant religious tradition, other times of its alter ego. Clearly there are sharp differences within Europe in this respect quite apart from continental contrasts—hence, to some extent, the different points of view expressed in this volume. Increasingly, the organization of health and welfare forms part of the same discussion—the more so given the pressures on the care-systems of all advanced economics as demographic changes take their toll. Faith based welfare, for instance, quite clearly exists on both sides of the Atlantic (as indeed do faith schools), but the discourse is different in each place. This rhetoric needs careful examination. A parallel theme can be found in the relationship between modern welfare institutions and their religious antecedents. The latter, including their associated theologies, condition the former—sometimes directly, sometime less so.

The final variation (Chapter 6) scrutinizes the links between religion and social difference. At the same time it continues the preceding discussion in that it introduces, albeit briefly, two further institutional carriers: first political parties and their relationship to social class (especially in Europe), and second the family and its role in the transmission, or otherwise, of religious ideas. The chapter starts, however, with social difference per se, recognizing that all societies mark this in one way or another—subtleties that are not easily translatable (multiple misunderstandings occur, some amusing and some more serious). Religion is implicated in these niceties, a point that becomes immediately clear in the anecdote in Chapter 2 about the dentist. The patient in this case was indicating his ability to pay a bill; the dentist was bewildered by the reference to religion as a proxy for financial security (see pp. 20–21). In the variation relating to these issues, special attention will be paid to the connections between religion and social class, and between religion and ethnicity. The increasing diversity in both Europe and the United States will be integral to this discussion—a topic which raises one of the most urgent political issues of the day: that of immigration. The final sections of this chapter turn, however, in a different direction; they look in detail at age (an increasingly important variable in modern societies) and gender. Here, interestingly, the similarities are as important as the differences. In practically every part of the Christian West, women are more religious than men and older people more religious than the young. The latter relationship, however, displays some interesting details, which differ not only between the continents but in different European societies.

Understanding the place of religion in both Europe and the United States is clearly an end in itself, but it is also a means to an end. More concretely a whole set of policy implications arise from this way of working, some of which have been referred to along the way. These will be gathered up in Chapter 7. They include, on the one hand, a wide range of domestic policies regarding religion as such, in both the private and the public sphere—policies, for example, that concern religious diversity, pluralism, and tolerance (and the difficult relationships between these). The American and European cases are very different in this respect, a contrast nicely captured in the following question: is religion part of the problem or part of the solution? Europeans are inclined towards the former possibility, Americans towards the latter. A number of external policies are also addressed, which themselves can be divided into different groups: those which relate to the building of Europe itself—notably the question of enlargement (including the case of Turkey); those which relate to the relationships between Europe and the United States, and the particular place of Britain within this; and those, finally, which relate to the attitudes of both Europe and the United States to the increasingly prominent place of religion in the modern world. Integral to the whole chapter is the notion of "alternate" or "multiple" modernities, a way of working which in itself has huge policy implications for the Western as well as the non-Western world.

The final section of this chapter collects the threads together, re-posing the crucial theoretical issue which can be summarized as follows: is Europe secular because it is modern, or is Europe secular because it is European? That in turn opens up the issue of modernity itself and its relationship to secularity. In short: is secularization intrinsic or extrinsic to the modernization process? If Europe is secular because it is modern, then modernization and secularization acquire an organic link. If Europe is secular because it is European, then the reasoning becomes quite different.

In light of the material presented in this book, we conclude that the latter is the much more likely option.

Who then are the authors? The first is Peter Berger, Director of the Institute on Culture, Religion and World Affairs in Boston. The Institute is a research center committed to the systematic study of relationships between economic development and socio-cultural change in different parts of the world. A better understanding of religion is central to this enterprise. The second is Grace Davie, Professor of Sociology at the University of Exeter in the United Kingdom and until recently the Director of Exeter's Centre for European Studies. In 2006, she completed a four-year term as President of Research Committee 22 (Sociology of Religion) of the International Sociological Association. The third is Effie Fokas, currently based in the European Institute of the London School of Economics and the director of the LSE Forum on Religion. Doctor Fokas is also the program manager of 'Welfare and Values in Europe', a project funded by the European Commission's Sixth Framework, and a research associate of ELIAMEP (the Hellenic Foundation for European and Foreign Policy) in Athens.

We are co-authors. All of us have read and fully endorse the book as a whole. Certain divergences in perspective are however recognized, and—where appropriate—are indicated in the text. Within this framework, Berger has been primarily responsible for Chapter 2 (which started life as a single authored article), Davie for Chapters 1, 4, and 6, and Fokas for Chapters 3 and 5. All of us have contributed at some point to Chapter 7. Mutual encouragement has been an integral part of our work.

Notes

1 See: http://www.bu.edu/cura/about/introduction.html (accessed 6 May 2008) for more details about the life and work of the Institute.

2 Canada, of course, is different again, and is not part of the following discussion. An excellent summary of the Canadian case can be found in Lyon and Van Die (2000).

3 The version reproduced here is the preliminary version; that published was a little different. We are grateful to *The National Interest* for permission to republish this piece.

4 Much of this work concerns the renewed assertion of Islam in global politics. The debate surrounding Huntington's *Clash of Civilizations* (1998) is a case in point.

5 Philip Jenkins's *God's Continent: Christianity, Islam, and Europe's Religious Crisis* (2007), is a welcome exception. Published shortly before this book went to press, it introduces a number of themes covered in more detail in the following chapters.

Chapter 2

Religious America, Secular Europe?[1]

It has become something of a cliché to state that the United States is a religious society, Europe a secular one. The cliché has been reinforced by recent events on both sides of the Atlantic, such as the role of religion in the last two presidential elections in the United States (i.e. 2000 and 2004), or the debate over religious references in the proposed constitution of the European Union. As a cliché is examined more carefully, the reality to which it refers is seen to be more complicated. But it also becomes clear that the cliché does indeed mirror reality

A few years ago I (Peter Berger) was having breakfast in a hotel in Austin, Texas. At the next table sat two middle-aged men in business suits, both reading newspapers. One looked up and said· "The situation is really heating up in the Middle East." He paused, then continued: "Just as the Bible said it would." The other man said: "Hmm" and went on reading his newspaper. The statement about the Middle East was delivered in the same matter-of-fact tone that someone in, say, Boston might say: "Just as Thomas Friedman predicted." Not long after this I was in a London hotel on a Sunday morning. I thought that it would be nice to attend an Anglican matins service. I went to the concierge, a young man whose name tag said "Warren" and who spoke with an unmistakably English working-class accent—clearly not an intern from Pakistan. I asked him where the nearest Anglican Church was, and for some reason added "Church of England parish." He looked at me with a blank look, then said: "Is this, sort of, like Catholic?" I said: "Well, not quite." He said that he did not know, but would look it up. The information he subsequently gave me turned out to be wrong. What impressed me, while he was rummaging in his computer, was not that this young Englishman evidently did not go to church. That is now commonplace in English society. What was more impressive was that he genuinely did not know what the Church of England was.

If one is to look more closely at this disparity, it is useful to let go of two widely held notions. The first is that religion is part of "American exceptionalism." America is indeed "exceptional," but with regard to religion it is very much like the rest of the world—namely, very religious.

The exception is Europe. (To be precise, western and central Europe; the Orthodox east is a different story. And "America" here refers to the United States; English-speaking Canada, as one might expect, is about half-way between the United States and Britain in terms of religion, while rapidly secularizing Quebec looks like a curious extension of Europe.) Most of the world today is characterized by an explosion of passionate religious movements. Europe is a geographical exception to this characterization. The case for this has been forcefully argued by Grace Davie, in her recent book with the telling title *Europe: The Exceptional Case* (2002). The other exception is sociological—a cross-national intelligentsia, which is indeed highly secularized.

The other notion to be discarded is that modernity brings about a decline of religion, a notion dignified by the term "secularization theory." Most sociologists of religion now agree that this theory has been empirically shown to be false. (I myself held to the theory until, beginning in the 1970s, the data made it increasingly difficult to do so.) The theory fails spectacularly in explaining the difference between the United States and Europe. It is hard to argue that, say, Belgium is more modern than the United States. Indeed, one could say that secularization theory was an extrapolation of the European situation to the rest of the world—an understandable but finally invalid generalization. It was helped along by the fact that theories are the product of intellectuals, who mainly talk to each other and who, like everyone else, tend to see the world from their own point of view.

Some time ago a German professor of my acquaintance gave some lectures at the University of Texas. He stayed at the faculty club and was thus protected from encounters such as mine in the hotel breakfast room. He felt very much at home—until Sunday morning, when he hired a car to explore the Texas countryside. He was bewildered by a massive traffic jam in downtown Austin, until he realized that it was caused by large numbers of people going to church. He then turned on the car radio and found that most stations were broadcasting Evangelical services. It then dawned on him that the faculty club did not provide an accurate reflection of American society (though, I assume, he went back to Germany and told everyone about exceptionally bizarre America). One might add that the same initial mistake could be made if one thought that the faculty club of Delhi University reflected the place of religion in India.

Intellectual curiosity is always aroused by exceptions. Explaining European secularity, especially its contrast with the United States, is one of the most interesting topics for the study of contemporary religion. But before I take a stab at this formidable task, it will be useful to go into some more detail as to what is different and what is, nevertheless, similar about the place of religion on the two continents.

What is Different?

Survey data show up the difference both on the levels of institutional behavior and of expressed opinion. Both Catholic and Protestant churches are in deep trouble in Europe. Attendance at services has declined sharply for many years, there is a shortage of clergy because of lagging recruitment, finances are in bad shape, and the churches have largely lost their former importance in public life. When people are asked about their beliefs—such as in God, life after death, the role of Jesus Christ as redeemer—the scores are low both in comparison with the past and with other parts of the world. The same is the case when people are asked whether religion is important in their lives.

There are differences within Europe. Broadly speaking, religious indicators are stronger in predominantly Catholic countries than in predominantly Protestant countries, though they point downward in both. Ireland and Poland have the highest indicators. Paul Zulehner, an Austrian sociologist, has described the Czech Republic and formerly communist, eastern Germany as the only regions in which atheism has become a kind of established faith. Still, it is fair to say that western and central Europe is the most secularized area in the world (Australia is the only other large area which may fall into this category). This has become so much part of European culture that the term "Eurosecularity" seems appropriate. Originally a phenomenon centered in the northern part of the continent, this secular culture spreads quite rapidly as other regions are absorbed into it. This was the case in the south, in Italy after World War II and very dramatically in Spain after the demise of the Franco regime. I would venture a prediction: countries are pulled into secularity to the degree by which they are integrated into Europe. This is already noticeable in Ireland and Poland. I doubt whether Eastern Christian Orthodoxy will provide immunity against this cultural penetration. The case of Greece would seem to confirm this view; it remains to be seen what happens in Romania and Bulgaria as they too are absorbed into Europe. (Russia provides a different picture, but this cannot be pursued here.)

As is often noted, European politics eschews the sort of religiously tinged rhetoric which is common in the United States. What is more important, Europe lacks the massive presence of Evangelical Protestantism, which is a crucial part of the American scene. Along with resurgent Islam, the most dynamic religious movement in the world today is Pentecostalism. A British sociologist, David Martin, estimates that there are at least 250 million Pentecostals in the world today. The Pentecostal movement originated in the United States in the early years of the twentieth century and continues to have markedly American characteristics, even as it has exploded globally. Europe has been barely touched by this explosion (with the notable exception of the Roma population, who have converted to Pentecostalism in large numbers).

The American picture differs sharply from the European one. Both behavioral and opinion indicators are much more robustly religious. Survey data on religion are always somewhat suspect. Given the respective cultural contexts, Americans may exaggerate their religiousness in response to survey questions, Europeans may exaggerate their secularity. Even if one makes allowance for this, the contrast is palpable. There are differences within the United States as well. The center and south of the country are more religious than the two coasts. And, at least since the middle of the twentieth century (things were different earlier, as we shall see presently), there has been an American intelligentsia much more secular than the rest of the population. This intelligentsia forms a cultural elite, with considerable power in education, the media, and the law. In terms of religion, India and Sweden can serve to mark the antipodes of religiousness and secularity. The American situation can be described as a large population of "Indians" sat upon by a cultural elite of "Swedes."

Two milestones in recent American history have been the Supreme Court decisions banning prayer in public schools and legalizing abortion as a constitutional right. This has enraged the "Indians," who have become politically vocal and organized in an unprecedented way. I think that much of American politics since 1963 (the date of the first Supreme Court decision) can be much better understood if one sees it as, in part, a struggle between the activists of these two groups. Most Americans are somewhere in the middle on the cultural issues being fought over by the activists, professing what Nancy Ammerman, an American sociologist, has called "golden-rule Christianity"—a somewhat vague and broadly tolerant form of religion. It so happens, however, that the two sets of activists have become important as constituencies of, respectively, the two major political parties. As a result, American politics has become marked by a conflict between religious and secular activists quite out of proportion in terms of the beliefs of most Americans.

What is Similar?

Modernity does not necessarily bring about secularization. What it does bring about, in all likelihood necessarily, is pluralism. Through most of history, most human beings lived in communities with a high degree of homogeneity of beliefs and values. Modernity undermines such homogeneity—through migration and urbanization, by which people with very different beliefs and values are made to rub against each other—through mass education and mass literacy, which opens up cognitive horizons unknown to most individuals in pre-modern societies—and, most dramatically, through the modern media of mass communication. Modernity has had this effect for a long time, but it is being rapidly diffused and intensified by globalization. In today's world one can find very few places that have been left untouched by this pluralist dynamic. Religion has been affected just like everything else. Pluralism transforms religion both institutionally and in the consciousness of individuals. Religious institutions, many of which had been accustomed to a monopoly status, now have to deal with competition. In effect, there emerges a religious market in which individuals can, indeed must, make choices. On the level of consciousness this means that religion is no longer taken for granted, but becomes the object of reflection and decision.

Such a religious market is obviously enhanced if many religious communities coexist in the same social space and if their freedom to operate is secured in law. The United States has had an obvious historical advantage on both counts compared with Europe. However, the pluralist dynamic begins to make its impact even in countries where one religious community continues to command the nominal allegiance of most of the population and where one such community continues to be recognized as the official religion of the state. France is an example of the first case, England of the second. While relatively few French people adhere to a religious community other than the Catholic one, Catholicism is certainly no longer taken for granted as the normal religion in the society, and individuals minimally have the choice of having little or nothing to do with it. In England there continues to be the legal establishment of the Anglican Church, but this has less and less influence in the lives of most English people. In both countries there is, in fact, a religious market with many options. In America the term "religious preference" has become part of the common discourse, tellingly derived from the language of consumer economics. The term may just as well be applied to the European situation.

What is similar, then, is the powerful effect of pluralism. Institutionally, this means that both Catholic and Protestant churches (in addition, of course, to the various minority faiths) must operate as voluntary associations, even if their theological self-understanding militates against this. Max Weber and Ernst Troeltsch made a classical distinction between the church, into which one is born, and the sect, which one joins voluntarily. Richard Niebuhr suggested that America has invented a third type of religious institution—the denomination. This is a religious institution with many of the characteristics of a church, but which (*de facto* if not *de jure*) recognizes the right of competing institutions to exist, and which is maintained by the voluntary adherence of its members. The pluralist situation forces all churches to act as denominations. Thus the Catholic Church in France, as elsewhere in Europe, is in fact a denomination. This fact is still quite repugnant to its official ecclesiology, but the Catholic Church has given a degree of theological legitimacy to the social reality by its affirmations of religious liberty as a human right since the Second Vatican Council. Thus the Church of England, rather less reluctantly, also acts as one denomination among others—and a minority denomination at that.

The loss of the taken-for-granted status of religion in the consciousness of individuals means that they are forced to make choices—that is, to exercise their "preference." The choices can be secular. They can also be religious. As we have seen, Europeans make more secular choices, Americans more religious ones. But even an individual who declares adherence to a very conservative version of this or that religious tradition has chosen to do so, must remember that fact, and will be at least subliminally aware of the possibility of reversing that decision at some future time. In other words, there is a huge difference between tradition that is taken for granted and neo-traditionalism that is chosen. The former, for obvious psychological reasons, is more likely to be relaxed and tolerant. Religious decisions can be passionate commitments (as in Kierkegaard's "leap of faith") or even trivial options of low emotional intensity. Either type is, in principle, reversible.

Thus, both in Europe and in America, there are large numbers of people who pick and choose from the religious traditions available on the market. Sociologists on both continents have noted and studied this phenomenon. Danièle Hervieu-Léger, who has worked mostly on French data, uses the term "*bricolage*"—loosely translatable as "tinkering", as when a child assembles and re-assembles the pieces of a Lego game. Robert Wuthnow, who has analyzed a mass of American data, calls the same phenomenon "patchwork religion." There is a difference, though. Europeans usually do their tinkering in an unorganized manner. Americans, with their deep cultural propensity to form associations, are more likely to tinker within this or that religious organization, including the formation of yet another denomination. A certain epitome of this is provided by the Unitarians, who define themselves, not in terms of any distinctive beliefs or practices, but rather as a "community of seekers." Hence the joke: how does the Unitarian version of the Lord's Prayer begin?—"To Whom It may Concern."

In recent years, on both continents, there has occurred a proliferation of "spirituality." People will say: "I am not religious. But I am spiritual." The meaning of such statements is not fixed. Quite often it means some sort of New Age faith or practice—believing in a continuity of personal and cosmic reality, reaching that reality by means of meditational exercises, finding one's true self by discovering the "child within oneself." But quite often the meaning is simpler: "I am religious, but I cannot identify with any existing church or religious tradition."

Grace Davie has described this attitude as "believing without belonging"—without, that is, belonging to any existing religious institution. It describes people on both continents. But there is also what may be called "belonging without believing," and that is more common in Europe. Another sociologist, José Casanova, has described the continuing public role of religion even in countries with a high degree of secularization. Take Germany, for example. There are no longer state churches and there is complete religious freedom. But all religious institutions registered as "corporations of public law" (which includes all but the most minor ones) have certain legal privileges. Among the privileges is the service by the state of collecting the (somewhat misnamed) "church tax." This amounts to eight per cent of the individual's income tax—depending on income, a considerable amount. An individual who does not want to pay this tax can simply declare him or herself to be religiously unaffiliated (*konfessionslos*) and thus instantly save quite a bit of money. Not surprisingly, many people have chosen to do this. What is surprising is how many—indeed the majority at least in the western part of the country— have not done it. When asked why, they give different answers—because they might need the church at some point in their lives, because they want the church to give moral guidance for their children, because they see the church as important for the moral fabric of society. Davie has coined another apt term for this phenomenon—"vicarious religion." This means that one does not want to be personally involved with the church, but wants it to be there for others or for the society as a whole. This attitude is rarer in America.

Why Eurosecularity?

It can be safely assumed that any important historical phenomenon will have more than one cause. There have been monocausal explanations of the difference between the place of religion in the United States and Europe—those, for example, that find the explanation in church–state relations or pluralist competition. While the latter two phenomena are plausible causal factors, they cannot explain the difference by themselves alone. Following is a list of factors which, I believe, should be given causal status. There may well be others. However, I propose that these factors, taken together, go a long way in explaining the exceptional character of

Eurosecularity, especially in comparison with the American situation. That comparison is crucial, not only because it helps to shoot out of the water the aforementioned secularization theory, but because the United States and Europe are the most important cases of Western modernity—to paraphrase Talcott Parsons, the "vanguard societies" of modernity. The differences between them make clear that there is no single paradigm of modernity—a matter of very great interest to non-Western societies on the path of modernization. The Israeli sociologist Shmuel Eisenstadt has written extensively about what he calls "alternate modernities." Following Eisenstadt, it is of very great interest in the Muslim world or in India if one can show that modernity can come in both secular and religious versions.

Separation of Church and State

Ever since Alexis de Tocqueville the separation of church and state has been used to explain the vitality of religion in America. Undoubtedly this is an important element of any explanation. Where religion is closely identified with the state, resentments against the latter almost inevitably come to include the former. Both in Catholic and in Protestant Europe, while there were always dissident religious movements, the major churches were officially established by the state. Well into the twentieth century the Catholic Church tried everywhere to maintain or to recreate this relationship by means of treaties ("concordats") with every type of government. Only the Second Vatican Council brought a significant change in this attitude. Lutheranism was established as a state church both in Germany and in Scandinavia. Calvinism did the same in the Netherlands, in Scotland, and in several Swiss cantons. By contrast, separation of church and state already occurred in colonial America, first as a practical matter (there were too many different churches for any one to successfully dominate), then as a matter of principle (as in the legislation on freedom of religion pushed by Thomas Jefferson through the legislature of colonial Virginia). The first amendment to the constitution of the United States, of course, made separation a keystone of the American republic.

Pluralist Competition

Institutions competing in a market tend to be more efficient than institutions enjoying monopoly status. A religious market is no exception to this. In Europe, even after the ties between church and state weakened in the wake of the French Revolution, people continued to view churches as a type of public utility. Such habits die slowly. By contrast, American churches, whether they first liked this or not, had to function as voluntary associations.

As was argued earlier in this chapter, the voluntary association is the social form of religion most likely to adapt successfully to the pluralist situation. Evangelical Protestantism today exhibits the most exuberant religious entrepreneurship (including that of the much-maligned "televangelists"), and this has much to do with its successes.

A number of sociologists, notably Rodney Stark, have recently sought to make pluralist competition the single most important explanation of religious differences between societies. They have done this by borrowing the conceptual apparatus of economics, from so called "rational choice theory." Again, as with church–state separation, this goes some way in explaining the difference between the United States and Europe. But it cannot explain all of it. Quite apart from the general difficulty of applying an economic theory to religion, this one must be selective in its choice of facts. Thus France has had a rigid separation of church and state since 1905—a not inconsiderable span of time. At least in principle, this opened the Catholic Church to the vicissitudes of pluralist competition. Yet this has not enlivened religion in France, which has been scoring high on any indicator of secularization in the intervening century. There is a curious aspect to this: just as secularization theory has been an extrapolation from the European situation, rational choice theory applied to religion has extrapolated from the case of America. But that is another story.

Two Versions of the Enlightenment

I am not a historian, but I suspect that the divergence at issue here sharpened in the nineteenth and early twentieth century. The roots, however, go back at least to the eighteenth, when two very different versions of the Enlightenment developed in Europe and in America. The historian Gertrude Himmelfarb, in her recent book tellingly entitled *The Roads to Modernity* (2004), distinguishes in fact between three versions— the British (in England as well as Scotland), the French, and the American. The sharpest contrast is between the latter two. The French Enlightenment was sharply anti-clerical, in parts openly anti-Christian. It was epitomized in Voltaire's famous cry: "Destroy the infamy"—the infamy being the Catholic Church. The French Revolution made a valiant effort to do so. It did not succeed, but what followed it was more than a century of struggle between two visions of France—one conservative and Catholic, the other progressive and anti-clerical. The latter won a decisive victory in the separation of church and state in 1905. Separation here meant something quite different from its meaning in the American constitution—the republic as *laïque*, thoroughly cleansed of all religious symbolism. This French ideal of *laïcité* influenced democratic thought and practice throughout continental Europe as well as in Latin America. The republic now claimed the ideological monopoly previously held by the church.

The American Enlightenment was very different indeed. In Himmelfarb's words, it expressed "the politics of liberty," as against the French "ideology of reason." The authors and politicians of the American Enlightenment were not anti-clerical—in any case, there was no clerisy to be against—and they were not anti-Christian. At worst (from a conservative Christian point of view), they were vaguely Deist. Thus the American Enlightenment could not serve as a legitimation of secularity in either state or society. Ironically, it has only been since the middle of the twentieth century that the federal judiciary, embedded in a newly developed "Swedish" intelligentsia, made decisions with a pronounced affinity with the French "ideology of reason." If one accepts Himmelfarb's account (I see no reason not to), the British Enlightenment was much closer to the American than the French version, which would lead one to assume that British religious history would more closely resemble the American one. It did not. Today Britain is almost as secularized as France. Other factors intervened, among them, very likely, the relations of church and state.

Two Types of Intellectual

Intellectuals (the term dates from the early nineteenth century) were the bearers of the Enlightenment. Because of the aforementioned difference, the intelligentsia took different forms on the two continents, secularizing in Europe, not so in the United States. There was also an important difference in terms of the influence of intellectuals—much more powerful in Europe than in the United States. Raymond Aron once called France the heaven of intellectuals, America their hell. This was certainly an exaggeration. But the United States has been from its beginnings a commercial and therefore a pragmatic society. It did not bestow much esteem, let alone power, on the "chattering class." Hence the telling American taunt: "If you're so smart, why ain't you rich?" This too has been changing, probably beginning with the "brains trust" of the New Deal. One may say, then, that the American intelligentsia has been "Europeanized," in its attitude to religion as in other matters. But this new American intelligentsia (lately also described as a "new class"), unlike its European counterpart, has had to contend with a strong popular adversary. (Needless to say, in the best tradition of Karl Marx, a relatively small group of American intellectuals have become "traitors to their class" and joined the adversary camp.)

Two Types of "High Culture"

Intellectuals define what is and is not "high culture." Given the differences already set out, European intellectuals have created a strongly secular "high culture." This has served as a sort of self-fulfilling prophecy, as more and more people outside the intelligentsia take their cultural cues from the latter. Thus in Europe to be modern, to be with the times as against being backward, has come to mean being secular. This was not the case in the United States—more precisely, not until recently. The "Europeanization" of the American intelligentsia must probably be dated from the 1950s, reaching its full force in the late 1960s and early 1970s. Today there is indeed an intelligentsia in America for whose members religion comes, if at all, in plain wrappers. This has led to a situation in which even the faculty club of a university in Texas is a place in which a secular European intellectual can feel at home.

Institutional Vehicles of Enlightened Power

Enlightenment ideas and enlightened individuals played an important part in both the American and French revolutions. But as the nineteenth century progressed—the century in which, I think, secularization began to develop fully in Europe   intellectuals as a class played very different roles on the two continents. As already mentioned, intellectuals differed in terms of their political influence and thus on the law. But there were two institutional vehicles of influence in Europe through which enlightened ideas came to be diffused from the intelligentsia to the general population. Both were absent in the United States.

One was the educational system. In most of Europe this was, and still is, under centralized state control. France is the clearest case of this—the curriculum controlled by the ministry of education in Paris, teachers (significantly called the "corps of teachers") trained in state institutions, then fanning out throughout the country. When primary, then secondary, education became compulsory, these teachers had unprecedented power to inculcate children in enlightened secularity. Unless there was a Catholic or Protestant school nearby, parents were helpless in the face of this indoctrination. Until very recently, the American educational system was under the control of local government. If un-enlightened parents did not like what teachers were telling their children, they could quite easily fire the teachers. This has changed somewhat, due to the increasing role of state government and teachers' unions, but local government still controls most of primary and secondary education in America. European governments in the nineteenth and twentieth centuries differed in the organization of the educational system, but on the whole they have been much closer to the French than to the American model.

Secondly, intellectuals played an important role in the growth of political parties and labor unions animated by various ideologies of the Left, mostly with a strong secular bent. There have been no analogues in America. Austria is a particularly clear case of this European phenomenon: the social-democratic Left built an entire subculture, within which party members could live from kindergarten to old people's home. This subculture was self-consciously anti-clerical and indeed anti-Catholic. The conflict between a secular Left and a religious Right was strongest in Catholic countries in Europe, though there were less sharp Protestant analogues. Only after World War II did there occur what could be called parallel processes of "secularization" on both Right and Left—the decline of the churches mirrored in the decline of an ideologically defined Left. But by then, as it were, the damage had been done.

Churches as Markers of Class

Finally, there are two explanatory factors present in the United States, both absent in Europe: first, churches are markers of class. The pluralism of American denominations combined with the high geographical mobility of Americans to produce a unique system of class symbolism. Thus in every American community there developed (and to a large extent continues to exist) a ranking of Protestant churches in terms of status. There are regional and local variations, but there is a very widespread rank order—usually with the Episcopalians on the top, followed by Presbyterians and Methodists, down to Baptists and other Evangelicals. American Protestantism invented a very useful instrument of status identification—the so-called letter of transfer. Individuals moving from, say, New England to the Midwest obtained a letter from their church certifying their good standing. Upon arrival in the new community they could show this letter to the local branch of the denomination. This not only certified the person in question as a good Methodist, Baptist, or what-have-you, but also indicated that he or she was an individual adhering to the bourgeois virtues of the "Protestant ethic." One could say that the letter of transfer was the first form of the credit card.

Max Weber understood this. In his essay on American Protestantism he recounted the story of a German dentist who had settled in America and who told Weber the following story. A new patient had come in, sat in the chair, and told the dentist which church he belonged to. The German dentist did not understand what church membership had to do with the man's teeth. What the patient was telling the dentist was clear: "Take care of my teeth. Don't worry about your bill. I'll pay you." My first teaching job was in the south. A colleague told me that he grew up as a Baptist but that now, having become a professor, he had joined a Methodist church. I already had some sense of the denominational status system, so I asked him: "Why not Episcopalian?" He replied: "No, that would be pushing it." There are some, much feebler analogues in Europe, especially in England, but nothing like the American confluence of religion and class.

Churches as Agencies of Immigrant Absorption

As masses of immigrants moved to the United States, religious institutions and the network of philanthropic services they spawned were very important in easing the immigrants' entry into life in the new country. The Catholic Church did this, first for the Irish and then for immigrants from southern and central Europe. The Lutheran churches (originally all organized along ethnic lines) did it for Germans and Scandinavians. Orthodox churches (still today ethnically organized) and Jewish synagogues performed the same function for co-religionists coming from eastern Europe. The identification of ethnicity and religion waned in many of these groups as they became assimilated, but there remained strong loyalties to particular denominations which persist to this day. Needless to say, there are few if any analogues to this phenomenon in Europe.

What of the future? Theoretically, it is possible to imagine dramatic changes in the place of religion on either continent or both. History is full of unexpected religious upheavals. In the early sixteenth century, say, a time-traveling, modern social scientist, with all the research apparatus of his craft, would hardly have predicted the religious earthquake of the Reformation a few years down the line. All one can say is that, at present, there are no empirical indications that Europe is becoming more religious or the United States less so. There is at least an intimation of a change in Europe, due to the massive presence of large numbers of Muslims who are unwilling to play by the rules of *laïcité*. Conceivably this might lead to a reassessment in the majority population of the Christian roots of the much-vaunted "European values." But here too very different scenarios are possible. For the time being, therefore, Europeans and Americans are well advised to come to terms with the great difference between the place of religion in their respective cultures.

Notes

1   As noted in the Introduction, this chapter is a slightly edited version of "Religion and the West," an article which originally appeared in *The National Interest*, summer 2005. Permission to republish is gratefully acknowledged.

Chapter 3

Variation One: Contrasting Histories

The first paragraph of Chapter 2 starts thus: "It has become something of a cliché to state that America is a religious society, Europe a secular one." A line or so later it continues: "As a cliché is examined more carefully, the reality to which it refers is seen to be more complicated. But it also becomes clear that the cliché does indeed mirror reality." This chapter represents a first attempt to reconcile this seeming contradiction. At the same time it constitutes our first "variation."

It begins by tracing the different histories of religion in Europe and the United States, concentrating on the factors which shed light on the current religious situation in each place. The cliché takes shape. The chapter then sets out a range of theories that attempt to explain these differences, paying particular attention to the relationship between context and theory. The cliché is explained. The third section revisits the data, appreciating that both Europe and the United States are diverse and complex cases. In so doing, the accuracy of the cliché is called into question—there are similarities as well as differences between the two. The final section, however, returns us firmly to base. Not only does it reaffirm the cliché, it argues that the contrasts between Europe and the United States have multiple implications. In order to appreciate these fully, two concepts are introduced: exceptionalism and multiple or alternate modernities. The latter is the more important—it becomes in fact a *fil conducteur* for this book as a whole.

Documenting the Cliché

Europe

In 1831, one of the foremost scholars concerned with religious comparison—Alexis de Tocqueville—made the following remark in a letter drafted on the outskirts of New York City: "Sunday is rigorously observed. I have seen streets barred off before churches during divine service; the law commands these things imperiously, and public opinion, much stronger than the law, obliges everyone to show himself at church and to abstain from all diversion" (Pierson 1938: 153–4). De Tocqueville sought to make sense of this strange (for him, a French European) situation of religious vitality with reference to the separation of church and state in the United States. A discussion of the different trajectories of religion in Europe and the United States has, necessarily, to begin with this point.

In what follows, however, the precise legal or constitutional connections between state and church in different parts of Europe are not the focus of the argument. They are, of course, important—crucially so—to the proper understanding of each European nation and its specific history.[1] So too is the manner in which the relationships between church and state change over time in different parts of the continent, the essence of Martin's classic analyses of secularization (see below). In this section, however, the emphasis will lie on the existence per se of a dominant church and the assumption that this is the "normal" form of religious organization in almost all European societies. Such churches can be Orthodox, Catholic, or Protestant. They are all, however, 'churches' in the sociological sense: that is, inclusive institutions into which you are born and of which you remain a member unless you do something specific to end that membership. They are, to be direct about it, the place in which your funeral will take place unless you, or someone else, suggests something different.

Historically, the case is clear: for centuries the presence of a "state" church has been almost palpable in European societies, even the most secular such as France. For most of the post-war period, however, it became harder to argue the case. The historic churches did not fit well into the much more individualistic rhetoric of the 1960s, a decade that undermined traditional institutions of all kinds, secular as well as religious. Unsurprisingly, large numbers of people (sociologists among them) began to assume that the twenty-first century would be very different: "state" churches, or their equivalents, would disappear—and sooner rather than later. Post 1989, however, there has been a further shift in perspective, prompted by the collapse of communism in eastern and central Europe. Fresh expressions of the "state" church re-emerged in those parts of the continent where religion had been proscribed for two generations. Clearly this was more true in some countries than in others—a "strong" to "weak" continuum can be drawn between, say, Poland at one end and East Germany or Estonia at the other—but the crucial point is clear. Here as in the rest of Europe, a historically dominant church (large or small, strong or weak, growing or shrinking, formally attached to the state or not) remains the assumed model. Religious minorities are treated differently: some well, some badly.

Exactly the same point can be made in terms of culture, where the story is more continuous. Right across Europe, the presence of the historic churches continues to be massively, if not always consciously, reflected in time (in the shape of the week and in holidays) and in space (in architecture, town planning, and place names). Such churches dominate both calendar and skyline. They are, moreover, territorial realities, manifested at every level of society. The church building, for example, can almost always be found at the center of town, from which the dwellings sprawl outwards—an important point of reference for most citizens, mental as well as physical; so too the administrative unit of which it was part: the parish. For much of European history, the parochial system was the cornerstone of both civic and ecclesiastical life, the more so given the extent to which these categories overlapped.[2]

Locality (territory) continues to resonate, both directly and indirectly. In twenty-first century England, for instance, simply to live in a parish still confers the right to be married in the parish church, a situation that is difficult to sustain in a diverse and mobile society. Further south, local festivals attract disproportionate numbers of people, taking European populations back to their roots on a regular basis. Spanish examples come particularly to mind and have been well documented (Albert-Llorca 1996). Parish churches, moreover, remain the repository of local memories (both individual and collective) all over Europe, which is one reason why their closure provokes protest, even if few people attend them on a regular basis (Davie 2000). Local ceremonies, finally, very often take place in or alongside the parish church—including the rituals associated with two World Wars and those who died therein. These are powerful reminders of the centrality of the parish church in European history.

Up to a point, the same process occurs at national level. Here too the historic church is a marker of territory as it is of national identity, the more so if reinforced by close church–state relations. Populations "belonged" to a church if they lived in a particular place; indeed in many respects, they still do. The Orthodox churches of eastern Europe offer the clearest example of this tendency, but it exists elsewhere – including, in more muted form, in the Lutheran churches of the Nordic countries. In most parts of the continent, such links are entirely benign—national churches are a source of pride for their populations and remain implicit markers of identity (almost all Finns, for example, are members of the Evangelical Lutheran Church of Finland). "Good" things happen in these churches: national ceremonies, public celebrations, and prominent funerals. Where else can these things take place? Less "religious," but equally important, is national heritage. Buildings such as Westminster Abbey in London, Notre Dame in Paris, or Cologne Cathedral attract hundreds of thousands of visitors—crowds in which tourists merge with pilgrims, and pilgrims with churchgoers on a daily basis.

There is, however, a darker side to the "national" church: one that showed itself all too visibly in the Balkans in the 1990s, when privileged churches allowed themselves to be instrumentalized in conflicts that rapidly became both violent and destructive. "Bad" things happened in the Balkans in the name of religion. Such episodes revive a problematic past: they remind Europeans of centuries dominated by "religious" wars, in which church and state, as ever, were inextricably linked. The struggle to emerge from this past is part and parcel of modernity as this is understood by Europeans. It lies behind the essentially European understanding of the Enlightenment as a freedom from religion, the focus of the following chapter. At the same time, it provides the rationale for a strictly secular state.

John Madeley, a political scientist, considers these connections in the long term, seeing the history of religion in Europe in terms of a triad of church, state, and nation, represented in sixteenth-century depictions of Europe with the triple crown adorning the continent. This triad constitutes three separate sources of power, which, in historical terms, function in a series:

> First, the church inherited part of its claim to universal dominion from the Roman Empire; then, after centuries of strain between religious *sacerdotium* and secular *regnum*, this claim was successfully contested and set aside by ever more powerful dynastic states and empires in the early-modern period; and finally, from approximately 1800, the claim of the nation to be the unique font of sovereignty and political authority has progressively been pressed. (Madeley 2003: 9)

Few people would dispute this understanding of European history whether they approve of it or not. An additional point is however important—one, moreover, that is fundamental to the argument of this chapter. State churches were not only powerful players in the history of Europe, they have, in addition, framed the terms of the debate. Or to put the same point in a different way, their influence on the mentalities of European populations is as important as the history itself. Vicarious religion—an idea to be discussed in detail in a later section of this chapter—derives directly from this past.[3]

David Martin engages the same debate. What currently exist in Europe are the remnants and mutations of an old story of Christian Europe and of Christian European nations. Martin describes this story through sketches of religion in Europe which "can be mentally superimposed like a set of transparencies" (Martin 2005: 78). He notes that Christianity in particular embodies a dialectic of the religious and the secular that generates secular mutations of faith rather than straightforward replacements and displacements. Within this context, religion in Europe does not function as a separate channel of culture but as a distinctive current which "mingles in the mainstream, sometimes with the flow, sometimes against." As a result, religious forms and molds are often reflected in secular analogues. A clear example, to be examined in detail in Chapter 5, can be found in the residues of religious patterns found in the welfare state across Europe. This is strikingly different from the American case. The consequence, moreover, is two-fold: the presence of the state church in Europe determines not only how people think about religion (see above); it can also be seen in the secular sphere. Hence, to give but one example, the comparatively greater expectations of Europeans regarding the state as a carer for its people. The notion of the European state church has leaked into the culture and discourse of the society of which it is part.

Clearly a church embedded in territory has, for better or worse, a particular place in European history. A church embedded in territory, however, is a static church—necessarily so. Hence the following crisis. The forms and structures of religion that worked so well in the long-term stabilities of pre-modern Europe, came under severe strain at the time of the industrial revolution. Rapid industrialization, and the equally fast urbanization that went with it, were devastating for institutional structures that were anchored in place. The onslaught came differently in different parts of the continent, but there can be little doubt that the profound dislocations that took place in Europe at this time were disastrous for churches in which the rural parish was central. Quite simply they were unable to move fast enough into the rapidly growing cities where their "people" now resided; as a result they increasingly lost their control over the beliefs and behavior of European populations. This was a blow from which these institutions have never fully recovered.

It is here, moreover, that the assumed link between modernization and secularization has found its *raison d'être*, a link embraced by the founding fathers of sociology and, almost without exception, those who followed after. Too quickly, however, the wrong inference was drawn: that there is a necessary incompatibility between religion per se and modern, primarily urban, life. This is clearly not the case. Something quite different happened in the United States, where—significantly—territorial embedding had never taken place; nor was this the case in the global regions of the developing world, in which some of the largest cities house some of the largest churches, not to mention tens of thousands of smaller ones.

But the shift should not be exaggerated even in Europe.[4] In many parts of the continent, the traditional model endured well into the post-war period, including—paradoxically—in France where it sustained an effective Catholic culture until the early 1960s. The collapse came late in France, but was all the more cataclysmic when it happened (Hervieu-Léger 2003). Something rather similar is now taking place in Spain some 30 to 40 years later. Elsewhere, the rural model had been seriously eroded for nearly a century, not least in Britain, where a different process occurred. Here, new forms of religious life emerged alongside the historic model, some of which grew as rapidly as the cities of which they were part. Both non-conformists and Catholics mushroomed in the nineteenth-century city, albeit for different reasons. The first filled the spaces left by the historic church; the latter catered for new sources of labor coming in from Ireland. In short what happens varies from place to place—careful attention to detail is essential if these processes are to be fully understood. Enough has been said, however, to indicate a distinctive European story in which the idea as well as the reality of a "state" church is central.

The United States

The process discovered in the United States is fundamentally different. So different in fact that it is best understood as a reaction to the European case—a reaction powerful enough to drive people across the ocean as they sought escape from religious persecution in Europe. It is for this reason that a "freedom to believe," as opposed to a "freedom from belief" is critical to the history of religion in the United States—a notion that very quickly became a foundational principle, at least in theory. Practice was sometimes different however, especially in the early days: seventeenth-century Puritans, for instance, persecuted both Jesuits and Quakers, and anti-Catholicism remained rife in the eighteenth and nineteenth centuries. Despite such lapses, the crucial point is clear: "religious freedom as a cornerstone, as part of the American founding history and its values, is a deeply felt and inspiring notion for most Americans" (Gunn 2004: 11).

Such freedoms were embraced in different, but interrelated, ways. The first is constitutional; the second organizational. The constitutional question resonates from the outset: as the separate states of the colonial period formed themselves into a new nation, the separation of church and state became embedded in the key documents—more precisely into two clauses of the First Amendment to the Constitution. These have become known as the "establishment clause" and the "freedom clause" and read as follows: "Congress shall make no law respecting an establishment of religion or prohibiting the free exercise thereof." Both are fundamental to American life and will be discussed in some detail in Chapter 5.

Equally important to that discussion is a parallel point: that is to recognize that neither sentiment prevents a strong link between religion and nation in the United States—indeed at times they encourage it. They also determine its nature. The link quite clearly is with "religion in general" and not with a particular faith, a sentiment nicely captured in the oft-repeated words of Dwight D. Eisenhower: "Our government makes no sense unless it is founded on a deeply held religious belief—and I don't care what it is" (Henry 1981). Exactly the same idea is evident in the many expressions of religion blended with patriotism that can be found in modern America—from the printing of "In God we Trust" on the currency to the addition of "one nation under God" into the Pledge of Allegiance. Indeed—and here is the paradox—it is precisely the separation of church and state that makes the interlinking of religion-in-general and national identity possible. It rests, however, on the assumption of a certain form of religious life—namely monotheistic, religious pluralism. Quite deliberately this has included Jews as well as Christians. To what extent it can embrace other world faiths is becoming an increasingly urgent question.

"Civil religion"—the diffuse connection between religion and national sentiment—has attracted considerable sociological attention. In its American form, the concept was famously developed by Bellah (1970).[5] Working from a Durkheimian perspective, Bellah sought above all to identify the features that bind Americans together. Prominent among these are the allusions to a shared Judeo-Christian heritage, taking care to emphasize commonality rather than difference. Hence the expressions found in the previous paragraph. Such phrases are consciously deployed by American politicians at key moments in American life, a fact abundantly clear following 9/11. They—and the ideas that they represent—are used not only to rally Americans behind wars and policies, but to increase support for the political system as such. A prophetic element can be clearly discerned, within which Americans become "God's chosen people," an idea which is not only disconcerting for many Europeans, but clearly open to abuse (Wilcox and Jelen 2002).

Religious freedom finds organizational as well as constitutional expression. With the partial exception of the Catholic Church, territory counts for little in the United States. It is replaced by two crucially important notions, both of which—like the constitutional clauses on which they rest—have become part of American self-understanding. The first is religious voluntarism: Americans choose their religious allegiance from an almost infinite variety of alternatives. The second is the congregation: that is the communities that emerge as a result of these choices, within as well as between denominations. Together, voluntarism and the congregation have constituted the common thread of American religious life almost from the beginning. In sharp contrast to the European territorial system, the local religious community in the United States is constituted "by those who assemble together (congregate) rather than by the geographic units into which higher church authorities divide their constituents, which is what 'parishes' historically are" (Warner 1993: 1066–7).

The evidence is everywhere, clearly visible in village, town, and city.[6] Here two examples must suffice. The first can be found in Nancy Ammerman's magisterial work on religious congregations in modern America (1997; 2005). Ammerman's publications reflect not only the variety but the sheer resilience of the congregational model, despite the multitude of vicissitudes which some of these people face. It is true that many congregations (perhaps the majority) confront decline, whether in the long or short term (1997: 44), but even the contents page of *Congregation and Community* (1997) gives an impression of persistence, relocation, adaptation, and innovation in combinations that would be hard to match in Europe. There is, in other words, more of a forward movement here than would be possible on the other side of the Atlantic and in an astonishingly wide variety of communities. Exactly the same feeling emerges from Lowell Livezey's work on the Chicago metropolitan area (2000); in the 75 congregations studied in this project, there is the same capacity for survival and adaptation to the surrounding context. Even more significant, perhaps, is the emphasis on how the congregations themselves "reflect, resist, or influence" the changes going on round them in order to be pro-active as well as reactive to what is happening in their neighborhoods (Livezey 2000: 6).

Livezey's work leads directly to a further point: that is the place of immigration as a significant factor in the evolution of religion in the United States. The links between religion and ethnicity will be addressed in more detail in Chapter 6. At this stage, however, it is important to grasp the role of religion in the United States as a fundamental category of identity and association. As a result, immigrant groups have, right from the start, used religion as a means for grounding solidarities and identities as they arrived in a new place. At the same time, the immigration of particular faith groups—for example Jews, Protestants, and Catholics from Germany, or Catholics from Ireland, Poland, and Italy—increased the sociological salience of religious identity in American life. Critically, immigrant congregations were not simply "transplants" of traditional religious institutions from their countries of origin (initially Europe); they became themselves arenas of social change, molding the country of which they had chosen to be part (Warner 1993: 1059).

More recent streams of immigration, following the passage of the Hart–Cellar Immigration Act of 1965, are both similar and different. The "new immigrants" are racially, ethnically, religiously, and linguistically less homogenous than those of the nineteenth century, and come mainly from Asia, Latin America, and the Caribbean. They have expanded considerably the religious diversity of America, bringing, for example, approximately as many Muslims and Buddhists as Eastern Orthodox. Nonetheless, the connection between religion and ethno-national identity remains central. Hence the common themes that can be discerned in this process: in the building of places of worship on the congregational model; in the emphasis on voluntary membership, lay initiative and participation in administrative functions; and in the use of worship sites as community centers. As in the nineteenth century, religion for the "new immigrants" becomes a means of coping with the challenges of relocation, of maintaining cultural and ethnic identities, and of providing important forms of assistance (Warner 1993; Ebaugh 2003).

In short, the history of religion in the United States reveals an entirely different trajectory from that found in Europe. Even more critically, it is an upward spiral: nation building, economic expansion, rapid urbanization, and an influx of new people interact positively to promote growth rather than decline in the religious sector. Each of these factors supports the others—a far cry from the vicissitudes of Europe's state churches in the same historical period.

Explaining the Cliché

Each situation—Europe and the United States—has produced a body of theory applicable to its own case. In Europe, the emphasis has been on secularization, an idea inextricably linked to the development of sociology as a discipline. In the United States, the stress has been on the market and the forms of theory that support a model of choice. Both will be sketched in the paragraphs that follow, paying particular attention to the relationship between the theory itself and the context from which it emerges.[7]

Secularization constructs itself as a master narrative, intrinsically connected to the process of modernization. More precisely, following two of its chief protagonists—Bryan Wilson and Steve Bruce[8]—secularization is linked to social differentiation, to rationalization, and to societalization, which together lead not only to a decline in religious beliefs and practices, but—much more importantly—to a decline in the significance of religion in the public sphere. Wilson, for example, perceives this shift in three areas of social organization: changes in the locus of authority, changes in the character of knowledge, and a growing demand that those engaged in the work places of modern societies should conduct their lives in accordance with rational principles. Rationality becomes in fact the *sine qua non* of the system. It is these mutually reinforcing transformations that characterize modern societies. Exactly how they occur will vary from place to place, but the underlying trend is clear, leading Wilson to an unequivocal conclusion: despite some differences in detail, "secularization in the West has been a phenomenon concomitant with modernization" (Wilson 1998: 51).

Steve Bruce's themes are broadly similar, but the style is very different. Both prolific and outspoken, Bruce demands that we pay attention to his thinking on this and other subjects. His writing is direct, clear, and punchy, and there can be no doubt at all about his position. The Wilson–Bruce approach, moreover, has characterized more popular writing in this field. Both in the academy and elsewhere, the "secularization thesis," including an assumed connection between modernization and secularization, has been the dominant narrative for the great majority of Europeans. Only recently has this begun to shift.

Casanova is less convinced. In what has become a classic text on the subject, *Public Religions in the Modern World*, Casanova "takes apart" the notion of secularization in order that the essential—and not always compatible—components within this term become clear:

> A central thesis and main theoretical premise of this work has been that what usually passes for a single theory of secularization is actually made up of three very different, uneven and unintegrated propositions: secularization as differentiation of the secular spheres from religious institutions and norms, secularization as decline of religious beliefs and practices, and secularization as marginalization of religion to a privatized sphere. If the premise is correct, it should follow from the analytical distinction that the fruitless secularization debate can end only when sociologists of religion begin to examine and test the validity of each of the three propositions independently of each other. (1994: 211)

It follows that secularization as a concept needs very considerable refining in order to enable a more accurate analysis of religion in different parts of the world—one which takes into account the different "propositions" within the concept itself. In other words, the connections between these factors must be considered case by case and country by country; they cannot be assumed a priori.

It is at this point that the links with the previous section become apparent. For Casanova, secularization as differentiation constitutes the essential core of the secularization thesis: "The differentiation and emancipation of the secular spheres from religious institutions and norms remains a modern structural trend" (1994: 212). It is not the case, however, that modernity implies necessarily either a reduction in the level of religious belief or practice or that religion is necessarily relegated to the private sphere. Indeed the intention of Casanova's book is not only to discover, but to affirm a legitimate public role for religion in the modern world. A second, and very relevant point follows from this: it is precisely those churches that have resisted the structural differentiation of church and state, which have the greatest difficulty coming to terms which the pressures of modern lifestyles. Hence the decline, relatively speaking, of religious vitality in much of modern Europe where state churches are more likely to persist—exactly as de Tocqueville had observed. This is not an inevitable outcome of modernity, but the consequence of the particular arrangements of church and state in one part of the West. It is a European phenomenon with a European explanation; it is not an axiomatic connection between religion and the modern world taken as a whole.

It is, however, a situation from which Europe and Europeans may find it difficult to escape, always assuming that they wanted to. The latter remark is important. Strictly speaking, "secularization" is a process subject to empirical examination in accordance with the norms of social science. It should be distinguished from the notion of "secularism," which—like all "isms"—is an ideology. All too often, however, the two become confused. More than this: the process of secularization becomes desirable precisely because it leads to secularism. Interestingly, in its earliest forms, sociology colluded with this notion. Auguste Comte, for example, worked on the assumption of a three-stage historical model. Society evolved from the theological to the metaphysical, before moving into the current scientific—with the strong connotation of "better"—stage. Understanding society, moreover, requires the application of "scientific" ideas to social as well as physical phenomena. Sociologists became therefore part of the secularization process that they are trying to describe. Nor have they entirely escaped from these associations. The assumption that secularization is a necessary part of modernization not only continues to exist; it is considered by significant numbers of social scientists to be a "good thing."

The connection, however, is very much harder to sustain in the United States, where almost everything is different. First the degree of religious vitality is striking, but second a whole new body of theory has emerged to explain growth rather than decline, abundance rather than famine. There are two main trends in this scholarship: first, the "new paradigm" for the study of religion in America, put forward in a seminal article by Stephen Warner in 1993, followed some four years later by more developed discussion; and second, the "religious economies" theory of religious activity, associated principally with Rodney Stark and William Sims Bainbridge.

Above all, Warner challenges the notion of a European norm. Rather than viewing American religion as an exception to or negation of the pattern of European secularity, he affirms the "institutionally distinct and distinctively competitive" status of American religion (1993: 1051). His approach fits well with the argument of this chapter: the European origins of the secularization thesis as opposed to the American genesis of the new paradigm are firmly endorsed (Warner 1997: 194–6). The beginnings of the two models go back centuries rather than decades. To be more precise, the secularization thesis, following Warner, finds its roots in medieval Europe some 800 years ago. The key element is the existence of a monopoly church with authority over the whole of society; both church and authority are kept in place by a series of formal and informal sanctions. It is, moreover, the monopoly itself which provides the plausibility structure—the authority is not only unquestioned, but unquestionable. Given the inseparability of monopoly and plausibility, the latter will inevitably be undermined by increasing ideological and cultural pluralism, a relentless process with multiple causes. Documenting this process, the gradual undermining of the monopoly, is a central task of sociologists, who quite correctly describe their subject matter (a meta-narrative) as the process of secularization.

The alternative paradigm, or meta-narrative, begins rather later—say 200 rather than 800 years ago and in the new world not the old, in the early years of the United States as an independent nation. Here there was no monopoly embodied in a state church, simply a quasi-public social space that no single group could dominate. All kinds of different groups or denominations emerged to fill this space, each of them using particular religious markers as badges of identity (religion was much more important in this respect than social class). Simply surviving required considerable investment of time, talent, and money, not least to attract sufficient others to one's cause in the face of strong competition. The possibilities of choice were endless, and choice implies rejection as well as acceptance. The affinities with the description in the previous section are immediately apparent.

Rational choice theory (RCT) takes this approach to its logical conclusion, drawing on two forms of theorizing in the social sciences. First on the economic ways of thinking epitomized by Gary Becker in *The Economic Approach to Human Behavior* (1976), which in turn derive from the utilitarian individualism espoused by Adam Smith; and second on elements of exchange theory taken from psychology, an approach initiated by George Homans and Peter Blau. What then are the implications for religion? Put very simply, the application of RCT to religion develops along two lines: it assumes on the one hand a purposive rational actor who is looking, amongst many other things, for religious satisfaction and, on the other, the existence of a religious market from which the actor makes his or her selections.

For many exponents of RCT, if not for all, the theory works in terms of supply rather than demand. Individuals are naturally religious—to be so is part of the human condition—and will activate their religious choices, just like any others, in order to maximize gain and to minimize loss. It follows that religious activity will be likely to increase where there is an abundant supply of religious choices, offered by a wide range of "firms" (religious organizations of various kinds); it will be likely to diminish where such supplies are limited. Other things being equal, enhanced religious competition in an open religious market will, necessarily, lead to a stronger "religious economy" and to greater religious vitality. The implications for Europe and the United States are clear: the former is characterized by a declining monopoly; the latter by a flourishing market. Readers are invited to draw their own conclusions.

RCT's strongest advocates are Stark and Bainbridge, Roger Finke, and Laurence Iannaccone, bearing in mind that many of the articles and books in this field are jointly authored. Between them this group of scholars have generated an appreciable literature of theory and counter-theory, matched by equally large numbers of empirical applications.[9] The details of this impressive body of scholarship lie beyond the scope of this chapter, except for one point. Here, as in the case of secularization, there is a clear subtext in the writing. For the advocates of RCT, the vibrancy of the American market is the "better" case—as opposed, for example, to the state-subsidized European churches staffed by "lazy," overpaid professionals. If the latter were subject to the rigors of the market, they too—like their American counterparts—would work harder, generating forms of religious supply capable of satisfying their customers. European churches, it seems, have only themselves to blame for their present predicament.

Who then is right and who is wrong—the advocates of secularization theory or the protagonists of RCT? Neither probably. The crucial point lies deeper and illustrates, once again, the essential difference between Europe and the United States in terms of religious understandings. More specifically, it lies in the fact that Europeans, as a consequence of the state church system, regard their churches as public utilities rather than competing firms. That is the real legacy of the European past. With this in mind, it is hardly surprising that Europeans bring to their religious organizations an entirely different repertoire of responses from their American counterparts. The majority of Europeans look on their churches with benign benevolence—they are useful social institutions, which the great majority in the population are likely to need at one time or another in their lives. It simply does not occur to them that the churches might cease to exist but for their active participation. It is this way of thinking which is both central to the understanding of European religion and extremely difficult to eradicate. It, rather than the presence or absence of a market, accounts for a great deal of the data on the European side of the Atlantic. It is not that the market is not there (it quite obviously is in most parts of Europe, if not quite in all); it is simply that the market does not work given the prevailing attitudes of large numbers in the population.

A More Complex Reality

Hence the complexity of the debate which must now be addressed in more detail. How, in other words, can we deal with the "awkward bits" that call the cliché of religious America, secular Europe into question. There are two ways of approaching this material. The first concerns the variations within as well as between Europe and the United States, some of which are considerable. The second relates to the accuracy of the interpretations presented so far. Is Europe as secular as it seems? And what about American religious vitality? Might this simply be a proxy for American sociability? Both questions—diversity and accuracy—will be considered in relation to Europe before turning to the American case.

Patterns of religion, and therefore of secularization, vary markedly across Europe—a point universally recognized among scholars of religion, but by none more so than David Martin. Discerning and explaining these patterns has been a central thrust of Martin's work for nearly thirty years, from his 1978 *General Theory* to his relatively recent "revisions." The former has become a classic in the literature. Secularization, in terms of social differentiation, took place to different degrees, in different ways and with different consequences across Europe, in accordance with differing historical circumstances. Mapping the "shapes" that emerge is a principal task of the sociology of religion. In a more recent volume (2005), Martin has updated the theory in a number of ways: not by altering the essential argument (that most definitely stands), but by taking into account significant—and in some cases unexpected—events in the past two decades. The collapse of communism, for example, was not anticipated in the earlier volume, nor the influx into Europe of large numbers of people, who brought with them markedly different forms of religious life. The "world" in many respects has arrived in Europe.

Much of Martin's thinking on the question of secularization stems from the contrast between "those countries, mainly Protestant, where Enlightenment and religion overlapped and even fused," and "those countries, mainly Catholic, where Enlightenment and religion clashed" (2005: 20)—a contrast from which two very religious cultures emerged, one of which is closer to the American model than the other. Much closer in fact, to the point of asking where the line should be drawn: between the

United States and Europe or between Protestant and Catholic cultures? The question becomes even more pertinent once the differences within as well as between the Protestant cultures of Europe are taken into account. Regarding the former, for example, two types of religious motivation can be discerned. The first is Anglo-Dutch or Anglo-American, and is based on the idea that religion can generate voluntary social capital, but in two ways: either as a passive service station under the shadow of establishment in the English style, or as something much more "active, entrepreneurial and competitive," as in America. The other type is more obviously "European" and exists in places such as Scandinavia and Germany. In the former are forms of social democracy which reflect the Lutheran monopoly, and in the latter a federal state that works in partnership with churches in order to maintain diverse forms of social assistance—differences that will reappear in Chapter 6 (Martin 2005: 77). In this chapter, the essential point is different and concerns the question of boundary. Is this, in other words, a question of "stepping westward" bit by bit, rather than two contrasting blocs: Europe and the United States? The question will resonate repeatedly in the material that follows. And in parenthesis, it is important not to forget the English speaking dominions—Canada, Australia, and New Zealand— which, on this as on so many other issues, lie between the European (more especially the British) and the American cases.

There are similar variations in Catholic Europe. Consistently, for example, Poland, Ireland (and in some cases, Italy) are identified as significant exceptions to the secular rule, with indices of religious activity that exceed those found in much of the United States, never mind in Europe. Why is this the case? In the first two of these, the answer is relatively straightforward: it lies in a particularly strong fusion of Catholicism and national identity. In both Ireland and Poland, Catholicism became quite explicitly an expression of the nation, not simply the dominant church; indeed without the Catholic Church, either or both of these nations might simply have ceased to exist. The Italian case is more complicated given the developed tension between the incipient Italian state and the Catholic Church in the nineteenth century. Here a whole range of factors must be taken into account: the specificity of Italian history, the presence of the papacy, and—particularly important in Italy—distinctive regional identities. Whatever the case, Italy remains markedly different from either France (the quintessentially secular state) or Spain (where secularization came late, post Franco, but then very fast indeed); so far Italy is resisting the European norm.

Catholicism, in fact, means very different things in different contexts. As Martin explains:

There is a socially concerned "reformed" Catholicism, particularly where Catholics are effectively a minority. There is an embedded folk Catholicism with its redoubts in the south, but with northern outliers. There is the ethnoreligion of eastern Europe, sometimes with recently renewed links to the state but energised by several different kinds of alien rule. Western Europe has also nurtured ethnoreligions, in particular in such niches as the Brittany peninsula and the island of Ireland. (Martin 2005: 77)

Quite apart from Catholicism, important sociological pressures can be discovered in this paragraph, each of which is worth articulating. They include the difference between majorities and minorities, the significance of regional as well as national identities, the difference between formal and informal theologies, and a "new" situation in eastern Europe where ethnoreligions have, once again, come to the fore. The list could in fact go on, illustrating nuance after nuance in the religious situation of Catholic Europe, never mind the continent as a whole.

The complexities are even more evident if the Orthodox parts of Europe are taken into consideration. Like Catholicism, Orthodoxy means very different things in different contexts—variations which pivot on two main axes: the relationship between religion and national identity, and the status of Orthodoxy as a majority or minority faith in any given context.[10] In the Orthodox "heartlands" (namely, Russia, Greece, Serbia, Romania, Bulgaria, Macedonia, and much of the former Soviet Union), the principle of *cuius regio, eius religio* has tended to prevail. In each case, there is a specific narrative (worthy of attention in its own right), but the common theme is a strong link between religion and national identity, bolstered by close church and state relations. This Casanova describes as the overlap between the imagined community of the church and the imagined community of the nation (Casanova 2006). There is little room in these imaginings for religious "others"—hence the tendency toward limited freedoms for minority faiths.

Orthodoxy outside these contexts is both a different and varied story. In London, for example, many Orthodox churches operate as hubs of national identity for various diasporic communities (be they Greek, Serbian, Russian, etc.). In some of these, debates develop between the "ethnically Orthodox" and converts over, say, the proper balance between English and the national language in the liturgy. Conversely in the smaller towns of the United Kingdom, communities of émigrés and converts often worship together in non-national or largely de-nationalized congregations. Different again are the Orthodox communities in places such as Finland or Albania, or even Poland, where the faith is practiced by a small part of the native population rather than by immigrants. Here Orthodoxy exists devoid of religion–nation and church–state links altogether. The latter cases are thus "freed," in Casanova's terms, to function more as religions of individual salvation than of collective identity (Casanova 2006).

Such complexities merge into a related but distinct question: is Europe as secular as it seems on first sight? The latter point can be approached from a different angle, drawing this time on the writing of one of our authors, Grace Davie. It involves three crucial concepts: "believing without belonging," "vicarious religion" (both of which were introduced in the previous chapter), and a turn from "obligation to consumption." The first of these, developed initially in the British case but then applied more broadly, captures one of the most striking features of religious life on the continent: that is the mismatch between different measurements of religiousness. There exists, on the one hand, a set of indicators which measure firm commitments to (a) institutional life and (b) credal statements of religion (in this case Christianity). Quite clearly, these indicators are closely related to each other in so far as institutional commitments both reflect and confirm religious belief in its orthodox forms. The believer attends a religious institution to express his or her belief and to receive affirmation that this is the right thing to do. Conversely, repeated exposure to the institution and its teaching necessarily disciplines belief.

No observer of the current religious scene disputes these facts–that is, that these dimensions of European religion are both interrelated and in serious decline. There is, on the other hand, considerable debate about the consequences of this situation. The complex relationship between belief (in a wider sense) and practice is central to this discussion, for it is clear that a manifest reduction in the "hard" indicators of religious life has not, in the short term at least, had a similar effect on rather less rigorous dimensions of religiousness —that is, looser and more inclusive notions of belief, alongside nominal as opposed to active membership. For the time being, both the latter remain relatively strong—the data are clear on this point. It is precisely this state of affairs which is captured by the phrase "believing without belonging" (Davie 1994), the popularity of which in both pastoral as well as sociological accounts of religious life in modern Europe indicates, in itself, its perceived accuracy.

The connections between emergent patterns of belief and the institutional churches are, however, complex. Not only do the latter continue to exist, they quite clearly exert an influence over many aspects of individual and collective lives—even in Europe—to the extent that some populations of Europe appear to "belong without believing." The notion of "vicarious religion" is helpful in this context. By vicarious is meant the notion of religion performed by an active minority but on behalf of a much larger number, who (implicitly at least) not only understand, but, quite clearly, approve of what the minority is doing. The first half of the definition is relatively straightforward and reflects the everyday meaning of the term—that is, to do something on behalf of someone else (hence the word "vicar"). The second half is more controversial and is best explored by means of examples. Religion, it seems, can operate vicariously in a wide variety of ways:

- churches and church leaders perform ritual on behalf of others (notably the occasional offices)—if these services are denied, this causes offence;
- church leaders and churchgoers believe on behalf of others and incur criticism if they do not do this properly;
- church leaders and churchgoers embody moral codes on behalf of others, even when those codes have been abandoned by large sections of the populations that they serve; and
- churches, finally, can offer space for the vicarious debate of unresolved issues in modern societies.

Each of these propositions could be developed at some length—both substantively and methodologically (see Davie 2000; 2007a). A full discussion goes beyond the limits of this chapter. Two points, however, are particularly important for the present discussion. The first is to appreciate the extent to which the notion of vicarious religion depends on the "state" church described in this first section of this chapter. The second follows from this in the sense that Americans find this idea almost impossible to grasp. The problem is immediately apparent in any comparative encounter— scholars from Europe and the United States "talk past each other," leading to a largely fruitless dialogue. What Americans call a "lazy monopoly" constitutes the core of the European system, entirely comprehensible on its own terms. Strikingly different are the responses of Europeans audiences (academic or other), who grasp vicarious religion immediately, despite the difficulties of language. Quite simply they "understand" what the concept is intended to convey.

This, however, is not the whole story. New patterns of religious life are beginning to emerge in many parts of the continent. Here, moreover, it is important to pay attention to Europe's diminishing, but still significant churchgoers—those who maintain the tradition on behalf of the people described in the previous paragraphs. In this constituency, an observable change is quite clearly taking place, best summarized as a shift from a culture of obligation or duty to a culture of consumption or choice. What was once simply imposed (with all the negative connotations of this word), or inherited (a rather more positive spin), becomes instead a matter of personal choice: "I go to church (or to another religious organization) because I want to, maybe for a short period or maybe for longer, to fulfill a particular rather than a general need in my life and where I will continue my attachment so long as it provides what I want, but I have no obligation either to attend in the first place or to continue if I don't want to."

It is this kind of thinking that lies behind an increasingly noticeable change in the membership in the historic churches, which become, in some senses, much more like their non-established counterparts. As Berger observes (pp. 12–13), voluntarism (a market) is beginning to establish itself *de facto*, regardless of the constitutional position of the churches. As such—it is important to remember—this pattern is entirely compatible with vicariousness: "the churches need to be there in order that I may attend them if I so choose." The "chemistry," however, gradually alters, a shift that is discernible in both practice and belief, not to mention the connections between them. Once again a full discussion of this mutation requires an article of its own (see Davie 2005; 2006b). It would include, however, a question directly related to the argument of this chapter— indeed of this book as a whole. It is this: if the churchgoers of Europe are increasingly organizing their religious lives in terms of choice rather than obligation, are they effectively becoming like Americans? Is this, in other words, yet another indication that the cliché set out at the beginning of this discussion is a whole lot more complicated than it seemed at the outset?

The answer is complex. There are in fact two religious economies in most European societies which, for the time being at least, coexist. The first is the incipient market just described, which is emerging among the churchgoing minorities of most, if not all, European societies, and in which voluntary membership is becoming the norm, *de facto* if not *de jure*. The second economy resists this tendency and continues to work on the idea of a public utility, in which membership is ascribed rather than chosen. It is the second economy that sustains vicarious religion which, for the time being at least, remains widespread amongst European populations. Observed sociologically, the two economies are in partial tension, but also depend upon each other—each fills the gaps exposed by the other. Experienced pastorally, the situation can lead to painful tensions for all concerned, most obviously for the religious professionals caught at the sharp end of different models of church life.

What then can be said about the American situation? The following remarks will reflect similar issues to those raised in the European case, but more briefly. The United States, after all, is but one country, not several (thirty or more in the broadest definition of Europe). The United States, however, is far from uniform from the point of view of religious life. For example, the characters described in Chapter 2—having breakfast or negotiating Sunday traffic—would have had a different experience in Boston or San Francisco. The former is in many respects closer to Europe than it is to the Midwest; the latter increasingly looks out across the Pacific. Europeans, moreover, feel "at home" in both, the more so if they enjoy walking! What emerges, in fact, is a map of the United States in which the further north and further "out" that you go, the less religion you are likely to encounter, particularly in its conservative forms.

Such patterns are clearly related to other aspects of American life— including politics—though it is important not to jump to conclusions. Christian Smith's recent work, for example, indicates not only the presence of a sizeable Evangelical constituency in modern America, but its internal diversity. Evangelicals may indeed have broadly similar aims, but they go about them in very different ways, which include diverse political choices (Smith 2000). Having said this, confessional clusters quite clearly emerge: Baptists predominate in the south, Lutherans in the north, and Catholics in the larger cities, notably Boston and Chicago. More will be said about these aspects of American life in the discussion of religion and class and religion and ethnicity in Chapter 6. It is clearly related to distinctive patterns of immigration over several centuries.

In this section, however, one final question requires attention: just how religious are Americans? It is a question hotly contested in the literature. In 1993, for example, Hadaway, Marler, and Chaves published their findings on American churchgoing in the *American Sociological Review*. The core of this article lies in the evident disparity between the data gathered from opinion polls (what Americans say they do) and the evidence assembled by counting the people who are in church (or an equivalent) on any given Sunday. Around 40 per cent of the American population declare that they attend church on a regular basis—that figure is surprisingly stable and frequently quoted. If, however, the methodology shifts to head counting of various kinds (as opposed to reported behavior) something rather different emerges. Using the figures assembled by these authors, it seems that "church attendance rates for Protestant and Catholics are approximately *one-half* the generally accepted levels" (Hadaway, Marler, and Chaves 1993: 742). They are, moreover, falling rather than rising. If such a finding is taken seriously, it makes quite a difference to how we think about religion in modern America.

Some five years later, the same journal ran a symposium on church attendance in the United States, gathering a number of responses to Hadaway, Marler, and Chaves. A wide range of issues were raised in these papers, some methodological and some interpretive. By and large the methodological issues are concerned with the data sets themselves (whether actual or reported) and their reliability. The interpretive issues are more interesting. Assuming that Americans do indeed inflate their reported levels of church attendance, what are their reasons for this? Why, in other words, do Americans wish to portray themselves as churchgoers and what does this tell us about modern America? And how does this compare with other populations, not least most Europeans?[11] The implications of these questions are fascinating and go straight to heart of the matter. They lead first of all to a reformulation of the question: is consistent over-reporting evidence for or evidence against secularization? It is evidence for in the sense that churchgoing levels are lower than most commentators had assumed. It is evidence against in that large numbers of Americans wish— for whatever reason—to be known as churchgoers. How then should we interpret these data? Two examples will illustrate the point. "I will say that I was in church last Sunday even if I was not" is, surely, indicative of a culture in which churchgoing is viewed positively. "I would be ashamed to admit that I was in church last week so I will say that I didn't go" reveals a very different peer group.

In focusing their attention on the gap between reported and actual behavior, Hadaway, Marler, and Chaves have opened up a crucial area of sociological enquiry. What emerges is paradoxical: in questioning the validity of the American data—that is the marked difference in religious activity between the United States and Europe—these authors reveal a far more significant difference, one that is qualitative rather than quantitative. Both, in fact, are important in a rounded picture of either/both continents. The statistics tell a different story in each case; so too do the default positions—that is, what is, or is not, considered "normal" behavior and by whom? The cliché once more takes shape: in the United States, churchgoing remains normal behavior; in Europe, increasingly, it is not.

Does the Cliché Matter?

That in turn raises the vexed question of exceptionalism. Which of the alternatives outlined above constitutes the expected mode of behavior in the modern world—and, always assuming that this can be determined, does it matter? Traditionally (in sociological terms), the United States was considered the unusual case, in so far as it appeared to be the only country in the West which continued to display high levels of religiousness. The challenge lay in trying to account for this "anomaly"—an explanation that could be found in the idea that Americans did indeed have far more religious organizations than most European societies, but this had more to do with American sociability than American religiousness. These, in other words, were essentially secular organizations. Bit by bit, however, the pendulum began to swing, as two things became apparent: first that

American religious institutions were quite clearly religious—vigorously so in many cases; and, second, that most of the modern world looked more like America than it did like Europe.

The change took place gradually, but by the turn of the millennium, most (though by no means all) scholars within social science had come to recognize that with respect to global patterns of religion, it is Europe, not America, that constitutes the exceptional case (Berger 1999; Jenkins 2002; Davie 2002). Europe, it follows, ceases to be the prototype. Or to put the same point in theoretical terms, the patterns of religion found in Europe do not derive from any necessary or causal relationship between religion and modernity, which will reproduce itself elsewhere in the world, but from the specificities of European history outlined above. The implications of this shift are immense—for policy makers as well as for social scientists.

All too often, however, debate in this field has degenerated into a problem already encountered: that is an unhelpful fight to the death between the protagonists of different viewpoints. Secularization theorists insist that they are "right" and that modernization necessarily implies secularization—in the United States just as it does elsewhere. In the short term, therefore, the United States is constructed as an exception to the secularization rule. Advocates of rational choice theory argue the opposite, maintaining that secularization in Europe is the result of a restricted religious market—the "solution" is simply a matter of time. Here too the exceptional case would, later if not sooner, give way to the norm. So far, neither side in this markedly discourteous exchange has been willing give way to the other. Hence the impasse identified by Casanova (2003), who—exasperated—has rejected the idea of exceptionalisms altogether, inviting instead a truly global perspective.

Such a view finds an echo in Shmuel Eisenstadt's much more constructive notion of alternate or multiple modernities—an idea already introduced and to be developed at some length in later chapters of this book. Advocates of multiple modernities recognize two very simple things: first that there is more than one way of being modern, and second that not all modernities are necessarily secular—indeed on present showing relatively few are. It follows that the United States and Europe should be seen simply as different versions of modernity, and for the foreseeable future at least are likely to remain so. If this is the case, social scientific thinking has a lot of catching up to do—this is one of the tasks of the following chapter.

One—not unrelated—point must be dealt with first. It concerns not only the presence of religion in any given society but how this is perceived. Once again it is Casanova who captures the essential contrast between Europe and America by asking the following question: is religion seen by its host as part of the problem or part of the solution? In Europe, according to Casanova, secularist assumptions have a habit of turning religion into a problem—the more so if it encroaches on public life. In the United States, the reverse is more likely to be the case—religion is not only vibrant, but welcomed as the source of essentially positive values. Such attitudes are applied externally as well as internally. Many Americans, for example, see religion not only as a solution to their own problems, but identify the lack of it as the reason for Europe's "decline" (including its demographic crisis). Similar proportions of Europeans, meanwhile, consider America to be dominated by religious excess and give thanks for their own secularity.

This, moreover, is nothing new. Some two centuries ago, the French Revolution found inspiration in its attack on the dominant forces of religion, the Catholic Church; in America, at more or less the same moment, the revolution was worked out through religion rather than against it. The philosophies that lie behind these contrasting positions form the essence of Chapter 4. Whether or not it is possible to envisage a more constructive dialogue—one in which Europeans can appreciate the position of Americans on these issues (and vice versa)—is a question to be re-engaged at the end, rather than the beginning of this book.

Notes

1 For a detailed account of the specifics of church–state relationships in Europe, see Robbers (2005).
2 The most obvious example can be found in the churches' role as the registrar of births, marriages and deaths—a system that endured in some parts of Europe well into the post-war period. The Swedish case is one of the most notable: the Church of Sweden was responsible for the registration of births and deaths until 1991.
3 Vicarious religion is defined on pp. 39–40.
4 A spate of recent publications affirms this point. Among them are Blaschke (2000 and 2002), Brown (2000), and Raedts (2004).
5 Interestingly "civil religion" as a concept comes originally from Europe—more precisely from the work of Jean-Jacques Rousseau. Latterly it has "returned" to become part of the current debate, both in Europe itself and in its constituent nations (see Davie 1994; Bastian and Collange 1999).
6 An excellent source for this material can be found at: http://hirr.hartsem.edu/research/research_congregtnl_studies.html, the website maintained by the Hartford Institute for Religion Research (accessed 6 May 2008).
7 Each approach has generated a huge literature. Outlines can be found in any standard textbook in the sociology of religion. Davie (2007b) contains a developed discussion of the relationship between each of these theories and the context from which they emerge.

8 Good examples of Wilson's approach to secularization can be found in Wilson (1969; 1982; 1998). Bruce (1996; 2002) continues the story.

9 Young (1997) offers an excellent introduction to the RCT literature which is developed more fully in a huge range of articles, notably in the *Journal for the Social Scientific Study of Religion* in the last two decades. These include theoretical discussions alongside multiple empirical applications of RCT.

10 This is a more nuanced approach than that offered in Chapter 1; it indicates a rather different understanding of Orthodoxy and its possible futures.

11 Hadaway, Marler, and Chaves (1998: 129) claim that a similar tendency can be found in Britain, though the indices are lower overall. Not all European social scientists would agree.

Chapter 4

Variation Two:
Different Intellectual Traditions

This chapter is concerned with culture rather than structures and deals with two major themes: the different understandings of the Enlightenment that can be found in Europe and in the United States, and the class of people—intellectuals—who are most responsible for the creation and transmission of ideas. The relationship between this class and the wider society is central to the discussion.

It begins with a series of references to the Enlightenment, emphasizing both commonality and difference in its various applications—an account which points immediately to a question raised in the previous chapter. Does the fault-line between Europe and America lie between the continents as such, or is this a rather more complicated alignment in which Britain at least finds itself closer to the United States than it is to Catholic, or continental, Europe? The issue cannot be avoided. Nor can the influence of the Enlightenment on the social-scientific study of religion, in the sense that this enterprise not only emerged in a particular part of the world, but is underpinned by a distinctive philosophical outlook—one, moreover, which is more rather than less hostile to religion.

The second section introduces the intellectuals of both Europe and America, probing their respective places in the societies of which they are part. Once again there are similarities as well as differences which will be illustrated with reference to both groups and individuals. There is also change. Paradoxically, as American intellectuals have become rather more like their European counterparts, some Europeans—in so far as they are beginning to "take religion seriously"—are beginning to move in the other direction. The implications of so doing will form a crucial thread in the argument. The concluding note forms a bridge to what follows; at the same time, it returns to the tension between culture and structure. The British case becomes an important example in this respect. Culturally it leans towards its Anglo-Saxon counterpart across the ocean; structurally—at least in terms of church–state relationships—it is pulled in the opposite direction, finding equivalents in the mainstream churches of continental Europe.

Exemplifications of the Enlightenment

Both the Enlightenment as such and the vast literature that it has spawned cannot be engaged in this chapter. The essential point—that is the very different attitudes to religion that can be discovered in its different manifestations—will be illustrated with reference to three sources: Gertrude Himmelfarb's *The Roads to Modernity: The British, French and American Enlightenments* (2004), Pierre Bouretz's penetrating contribution to one of the Berlin workshops that lie behind this book (2001; see also Bouretz 2000), and a fascinating vignette from Italy selected to illustrate a distinctively Catholic Enlightenment (Mazzotti 2001; 2007). The latter is important, as it reveals that the differences in question cannot simply be reduced to a Catholic–Protestant dichotomy.

Himmelfarb's "Roads to Modernity"

The Roads to Modernity: The British, French and American Enlightenments was published in 2004. It is an innovative, controversial, and widely reviewed book: some like it, some do not. Himmelfarb's essential claim is the following: that the French Enlightenment (based on reason) has been vastly overrated, at the expense of the British and American variants which have much more in common. Both the British, characterized by virtue, and the American, characterized by political liberty, must be restored to their rightful position, not only in terms of the historical account but with reference to their influence on modern political thinking. One point is immediately clear: this is not a dispassionate book. In writing what she calls a "revisionist history," Himmelfarb is reclaiming the ground for a distinctively American story. She insists, more precisely, that the American Revolution owes little to its French counterpart, and—as a result—has given birth to a very different, much more positive, model of democracy.

Himmelfarb herself is a well-known neo-conservative in her own society, a fact that colors reactions to this book. Those who do not share her political views will see in her writing a markedly selective account which omits the less savoury elements of the Anglo-American story (a fuller record of the slave trade for example), whilst emphasizing the negative aspects of the French experience (the brutality of the post-revolutionary Terror). There is truth in these accusations. They do not, however, detract from the essential point which concerns the place of religion in these various configurations. If it is clear, on the one hand, that the French Enlightenment constructed itself in opposition to the Catholic Church, a formidable institution in its own right, American aspirations were very different. In the latter, the Enlightenment—and the Revolution associated with it—saw in religion (more precisely in multiple versions of voluntarist Christianity) a vehicle for its own ideas. Multiplicities of religious organizations became an expression of political liberty, not its obverse.

Why was this so? The reasons are closely linked to David Martin's analyses of secularization, introduced in Chapter 3. To take the French case first, Martin explains in some detail both the growth and the subsequent clash of two quasi-monopolies: one Catholic and one secular. In France, as indeed in Catholic Europe as a whole, the church had resisted the Reformation, thus precluding the possibility of reform—more precisely of de-clericalization—from the inside.[1] As a result, opposition to Catholicism gathered outside rather than inside the church and became political rather than religious, linking arms with the currents of Enlightenment thinking already present in France. Freedom from religion—that is freedom from both beliefs and the disciplines of the Catholic Church (Voltaire's famous "*écrasez l'infâme*")—became a rallying cry of the revolutionaries. The "battle" persisted throughout the nineteenth century, culminating in a notably acrimonious separation of church and state in 1905 (Poulat 1987). Twenty-first-century commemorations of this iconic moment in the evolution of France indicate its continuing importance for French self-understanding.

The British story is quite different. It is true that the British had experienced a revolution which included regicide, but this happened more than a century earlier than it did in France. It involved, moreover, competing versions of Protestant conviction, rather than a straight religious–secular split. England had been Protestant since the Reformation, rather differently from her continental neighbours, but Protestant nonetheless. Scotland where Calvinism rather than Anglicanism provided the cultural codes—even more so. Hence, in both cases, there was a substantially de-clericalized church, and, in consequence, a marked absence of politically motivated anti-clericalism—a concept almost unknown in Britain. What emerges is different in each of the constituent nations of the United Kingdom, but in all of them both political regime and the populace in general accepted a far greater degree of religious pluralism—and in the fullness of time, of religious toleration—than was possible in the French case. Increasingly, albeit unevenly, Britain welcomed the presence of different religious communities as an integral part of the democratic process.

How then does Himmelfarb deal with these issues? In the British case, her reading of the Enlightenment is distinctly innovative. An example can be found in her claim that John Wesley—the founder of Methodism, high Tory and fierce opponent of the American Revolution—was essentially an Enlightenment figure. In support of her position, Himmelfarb stresses both Wesley's own intellectual sensibilities and his commitment to the education of the poor. Not everyone will be convinced. Nor will all her readers accept the inclusion of Edmund Burke within the Enlightenment frame. In this case, Himmelfarb emphasizes Burke's "powerful moral imagination" (2004: 92), his advocacy of public virtue (for her, a linking thread), and his critique of British excesses in India. All three points deserve consideration; taken together they counter at least to some extent his much better-known denunciation of the radicals across the Channel— which, according to Himmelfarb, was well justified.

Convinced or not by these inclusions, the essential question remains the same: where is the step change in this debate? Is it between France and Britain, or between Britain and the United States? Himmelfarb quite definitely locates it between France and Britain: hence her desire to rehabilitate the British Enlightenment at the expense of the French. It is equally clear, however, that you cannot simply move from Britain to the United States without appreciating the fundamentally different position of religion in American society—hence the contrasts outlined in the previous chapter. American acceptance of religion goes considerably further than the de facto toleration found in Britain. Right from the start, a "freedom to believe" becomes the motivating force of both the American Enlightenment and the American Revolution; that force, as a significant political movement, is not found in Europe.

Thesis, Antithesis and Synthesis: The German, French and American Enlightenments

In many respects, Pierre Bouretz covers similar ground, but he starts from a German rather than a British perspective. Three cases are outlined in his paper: Germany, France, and the United States, each of which becomes a distinctive model of secularity. More precisely, he understands these three cases as a German thesis, a French antithesis, and an American synthesis.[2] As ever, a long-term historical perspective becomes the key to understanding this process. Equally important for Bouretz is a linguistic sensitivity, in the sense that the distinctiveness of each case is often captured in a particular word which is difficult to translate: cultures create words to express what is important and relevant to them.

The process begins with the Reformation—in the casting off of the authority of the church by the Protestant reformers, recognizing that the revolt against both the despotism of the church and the dogmatism of the law is not a revolt against religion as such, but a return to the sources of Christianity. Hence in the German case, the emphasis is placed both on the individual believer and on the community of which he or she is part, which is independent from civil or political society. The significance of the former is captured by one of Bouretz's key words—the German notion of "*Bildung*," meaning a process of *individual* formation through the experience of life, of which Goethe's *Wilhelm Meister's Lehrjahre* offers the classic example. A particular understanding of both freedom and sovereignty follows from this: it resides in a respect for the autonomy of the individual that is both prior to and independent from political understandings the term. Hence a marked degree of hostility to the explicitly political model of the French Enlightenment.

The French process is, indeed, different. The essential point was made in the previous section: that is, the lack of a successful Reformation which leads in turn to a political revolt against religion as such. Here Himmelfarb, Bouretz, and Martin are clearly in agreement. An additional remark is however important: Bouretz emphasizes the emergence of the state as the "peacemaker par excellence" in the French case. The pre-eminence of this role dates from the seventeenth century, in so far as only the state can overcome the violence of religious conflicts.[3] Hence—from this moment on—the two protagonists in the struggle which dominates French history: on the one hand, an unreconstructed and hegemonic church, and on the other, a state that claims for itself moral as well a political authority. The ascendancy of one implies the decline of the other—this is a zero sum game.

Once again, an additional contrast is captured in a subtle, but crucial difference in vocabulary. In German, *Die Aufklärung* quite clearly introduces the idea of reason, but not at the expense of religious belief; the French notion of *les lumières* on the other hand, challenges not only the religious institution, but the worldview associated with it.[4] The radicalism of the French Enlightenment stems from this double attack. Here, moreover, is the root of a continuing ambiguity in the French case: despite—from the time of the Revolution the recognition of religious freedom as such (a right granted to both Jews and Protestants after centuries of persecution), there is continued mistrust of religion per se. The dilemma has never been fully resolved; it can still be seen in the attitudes of the French towards less conventional forms of religion (sects and new religious movements) and in the banning of religious symbols in public life. It will be discussed in more detail in later chapters.

Hence a third key word: the quintessentially French notion of *laïcité*. It, more than any other, is untranslatable, the reason being that almost no other European society requires a word that underlines with such clarity the absence of religion from the public sphere. A notable exception is Turkey—itself modeled on the French case, and in which the public presence of religion also causes trouble. The fact that France opposes the entry of Turkey into the European Union with more vehemence that most other European societies is simply one more paradoxical turn in this clearly unfinished story.

How then does Bouretz envisage the American synthesis? Here the timing is crucial: the United States of America came into being two centuries after the Reformation but at the height of the discussion about political freedom in its modern sense. As a result, the founding fathers of America—themselves Protestants—were committed to both religious and political freedom. This is distinct from the French case, in that these two ideas are seen as compatible with each other; it is distinct from the German example in the sense that privacy is given a higher status than "*Bildung*." The state in fact exists as much to protect privacy as it does to promote freedom. Once again this results in a continuing ambiguity best expressed as a question: how is it possible to protect the privacy of one, without—at times—jeopardizing the freedom of another (a distinctively American dilemma)? Each system, in Bouretz's analysis, carries with it associated dangers. But for Americans the key point is clear: religious autonomy becomes the model of political citizenship. It follows that good government implies not the unified state beloved of the French, but a plurality of interests, opinions, and powers, each of which balances the others.

Maria Gaetana Agnesi: Mathematics and the Catholic Enlightenment

One thing that emerges from the previous examples is the crucial difference between a Protestant and a Catholic culture. This is hardly surprising given the consequences of the Reformation for both the beliefs and structures of the church. An institution de-clericalized from the inside found itself in a entirely different position from one that faced, two centuries later, political rather than theological opposition. It would be wrong, however, to conclude from this discussion that there were no possibilities for Enlightenment within as well as against Catholicism.

The fascinating, and at times very poignant, case of Maria Gaetana Agnesi makes this very clear. Agnesi was a distinguished eighteenth-century mathematician—the author of a widely read treatise on calculus that appeared in Milan in 1748. She was also a pious and increasingly committed Catholic, dedicating much of her life both to her own devotions and to the care of the poor. Massimo Mazzotti provides a sociological account of this story, underlining two very interesting features: first that the scientific and Catholic dimension of Agnesi's life were by no means incompatible; and second that the explanation for this unusual mix of talents lies at least in part in the specificity of the circumstances that occurred in northern Italy in the mid-eighteenth century (Mazzotti 2001; 2007).

Here there was space not only for a Catholic intellectual as such, but also for a woman.[5]

Agnesi's *Cielo Mistico* offers the key to her personal views.[6] For Agnesi, mystic contemplation did not imply a rejection or negation of the power of the intellect. The latter was simply the first—and in itself inadequate—stage in a continuing process. "Enlightening clarity" must give way to "burning clarity" as simple cognition cedes to love. There was, in other words, "cooperation rather than opposition between the two faculties: while 'the human mind contemplates in marvel' the virtues of Christ, 'the heart imitates them with love'" (Mazzotti 2001: 673). The second point follows from this. In expressing these sentiments, Agnesi finds her place in a particular movement—one that takes place before what Mazzotti calls the "high season" of the Italian Enlightenment. Prior to the latter, a distinctive group of intellectuals gathered in Milan—a community that sought to promote modern scientific insights within, rather than in opposition to, the Catholic system of knowledge. Hence the possibility that mathematical analysis could become a tool, rather than an impediment, in the spiritual life of the believer. With this in mind, Mazzotti identifies the cluster of factors that, alongside her clearly ambitious father, explain Agnesi's remarkable success:

> A wealthy family eager for social enhancement, a Church eager for new charismatic figures, and a reformist religiosity characterized by favourable views about the education of women and intellectual achievement: these were the conditions that made it possible for Agnesi to establish herself as a legitimate author of a mathematical treatise and as an advisor to the archbishop of Milan on theological matters. (Mazzotti 2001: 683)

These conditions very largely disappeared by the end of the century. Quite apart from anything else, it was a long time before a woman, let alone an actively Catholic woman, would once again be offered a chair in a European university.

The Enlightenment and Social Science

Plainly the Enlightenment was not "one thing"; it was made up a many different contributions in several different places and over a long period of time. No doubt the pendulum will continue to swing between those who underline the essential unity of the movement and those who emphasize its diversity. That said, it is clear that some readings of the Enlightenment rather than others, furnished the philosophical foundations for the early social scientists. The point has already been made with reference to Auguste Comte (p. 33), for whom to be "modern" meant to leave both God and the supernatural behind. These unworldly attributes are replaced by the natural and the scientific, which become the primary—indeed the definitive—modes of explanation for the modern person. Hence the emergence of a distinctive epistemology, which embodied above everything else a notion of the future that was realizable through human agency. Epistemologies, however, very frequently turn into ideologies: a mutation in which religion is seen as not only irrelevant (something to be left behind), but damaging both to modern societies themselves and to the scientific study of them.

The process should not be oversimplified. Each one of the founding fathers of sociology, for example, paid close attention to religion. They did this in very different ways, but all four—Karl Marx, Max Weber, Emile Durkheim, and Georg Simmel—recognized the significance of religion as an integral factor in the upheavals taking place in Europe in the nineteenth and twentieth centuries. Integral yes, but unlikely to endure, at least in its existing forms. The twin processes of industrialization and urbanization would, sooner or later, erode the power of religion—a process welcomed by Marx, rather less so by the others, who wondered what might emerge to replace this. There was no doubt, however, about the outcome: modern societies were envisaged, for good or ill, as secular societies. This assumption sinks deeply into the consciousness of European intellectuals, among them social scientists. Its consequences are both direct and indirect: among the former can be found a marked reluctance to take religion seriously (it is not worth bothering about); among the latter (when the former policy fails) a pervasive tendency to construct it as a problem—something, in other words, to be overcome.

It is precisely this combination that characterizes the present moment in Europe. The particular episodes that have demanded that, once again, we do pay attention to religion—European enlargement, the debates surrounding the preamble to the constitution, renewed discussion about the freedom of speech (the Rushdie controversy, the murders of Pim Fortuyn and Theo van Gogh, and the Danish cartoons of Mohammed), the *affaire du foulard*, and the bombings in Madrid and London—will be spelled out in more detail both below and in Chapter 6. At this stage, a single remark will suffice: the re-emergence of religion in public life in Europe, and indeed anywhere else, was not anticipated. Europeans, including social scientists, did not expect this to happen; they were, therefore, ill-prepared to deal with it for the reasons set out above.

The Place of the Intellectual in Religious Debate

Peter Berger describes the United States as "a large population of 'Indians' sat upon by a cultural elite of 'Swedes'" (p. 12). How does this compare with Europe? As ever Europe varies. In parts of the continent, prominent intellectuals continue to be lionized—most obviously in France; elsewhere very much less so. There is no room in British society, for example, for a Jean-Paul Sartre or a Pierre Bourdieu; British society is much more like America in its admiration for doers rather than thinkers. But not all intellectuals are the same. In France, for example, there is no place for a species that exists in considerable numbers in Germany—the professional theologian. Nor, with the exception of Strasbourg, is it possible to imagine in France, the faculties of theology (some denominational and some less so) that can be found in almost every other country in Europe. Indeed at a meeting of a newly constructed European network concerned with the teaching of religion in the "new Europe,"[7] it became clear that northern European assumptions about the non-confessional teaching of religion in higher education were not always shared by their counterparts further south. Here—quite clearly—old habits (confessional teaching in confessional institutions) die hard, the more so in those parts of Europe where the teaching of or about religion is only just emerging after several decades in the wilderness.

But in which direction is Europe moving: towards greater secularity, or not, or in more than one direction at once? The debates surrounding a reference to religion in the preamble to the proposed European Constitution (2004) provide a useful touchstone in this respect. The question was simple enough: should the preamble contain a specific reference to Christianity or was such a reference no longer appropriate in the twenty-first century? At one level, the answer is straightforward: it all depends on what you think a preamble should be. If a preamble is concerned with historical fact, then the reference must be specific—Christianity, amongst other things, has had a huge and lasting influence in the formation of Europe. It is willful to pretend otherwise. But if a preamble is an inspiration for the future, the answers might well be different—or at least there are different questions to consider. Much of the confusion surrounding this highly controversial issue lay in the fact that Europeans omitted to consider the precise nature of the preamble that they were trying to write.

Two further remarks are necessary with respect to this episode. First the fact that the dispute about the place of religion in the preamble took place at all is as significant as its eventual outcome—most Europeans did not expect a controversy such as this for the reasons discussed above. Second the "patterns" that emerged as different countries took different positions regarding the reference to Christianity in the preamble demand our close attention—new configurations appeared as the countries that became part of the European Union in May 2004, most notably Poland, began to flex their muscles. "Old Europe" conversely was taken by surprise as the secular assumptions of France in particular were seriously challenged. In this case, the secularists "won"—there was no specific reference to Christianity in the draft agreed in 2004—but the sharpness of the opposition came as something of a surprise (Schlesinger and Foret 2006). Berger's prediction (p. 11) that increasing secularity will follow from inclusion in the European ambit may or may not be case. Interestingly, the papers drawn together in Byrnes and Katzenstein (2006) address precisely this issue. These authors are not altogether optimistic: as the European Union extends its boundaries, they argue that religious factors are not only growing in importance but constitute stumbling blocks rather than stepping stones towards greater integration.

Examining Unbelief

A related, but rather different, point requires attention: the study of religion in any given society must include the study of its secular elites. More precisely, it must look carefully at the ways in which these sections of society (the opinion-formers) respond, or fail to respond, to religious issues—the more so given the renewed prominence of religion in public debate. The need for such knowledge reveals, however, an underlying lacuna. Standard enquiries about religion have very largely omitted to include within them the study of unbelief, bearing in mind its considerable diversity. Unbelievers are not simply those who tick the "none" or "no belief" category in the questionnaire, but a complex continuum that includes at one end the convinced, articulate, and at times vehement atheist, and at the other, the mildest of agnostics. The line between agnostic indifference and believing indifference is fuzzy to say the least. Atheists, conversely, know a great deal about the God(s) in whom they do not believe: they also take on the characteristics of the society of which they are part. In western Europe, two very different European countries exemplify this tendency: the first, unsurprisingly is France; the second Norway. The situation in France has already been described: here unbelief not only becomes the alter ego of Catholicism, with its own symbols and legitimating narrative, it also sinks much deeper into the population than is the case elsewhere. In Norway, in contrast, the surprisingly large number of humanists in the population exhibit the characteristics of the majority church—paradoxically in some respects. The relatively wealthy Norwegian Humanist Association, for instance, is supported by the equivalent of "church" tax. Its members express their views firmly, but with considerable respect for others. In short, they are *Norwegian* humanists.

In eastern Europe—where atheism became part of the dominant ideology—something rather different has happened. Once again, however, distinctive patterns emerge. In those parts of post-communist Europe dominated by Protestantism, the years under Soviet domination brought about a collapse in belief, as well as in the institutional churches. In Estonia, for example, and even more notably in the former East Germany, unbelief is now the majority position. Berger is entirely correct to designate Berlin as the capital of secularism as well as secularity.[8] Conversely—and for reasons that require detailed examination—the Catholic Church was much more able to resist the communist onslaught. Indeed the contrast between East Germany and Poland, two neighboring countries, is dramatic in this respect. The Orthodox world is more varied: Bulgaria and Romania, for instance, present very different cases—the first is moderately secular, the second very much less so. Nor is it easy to say how, in religious terms, these countries will develop as they begin their membership of the European Union. Only time will tell.

We can conclude this discussion with a brief comparison with the American case. Unbelief in Europe is varied, but remains a significant element in most countries; it is growing rather than shrinking. In the United States, it is also growing, but from an infinitesimally small base. Why, then, is the number of unbelievers in America so small? Might one clue lie in the relationship between the religious and the secular already described—that is, that in many respects, the secular sections of European societies take on the characteristics of the dominant church in question? But in the United States there is no dominant church. Who then constitutes the opposition, or the alter ego of the secular elite? It is clear that many Americans observe with disquiet the growing dominance of the Evangelical constituency, the more so in so far as Evangelicals, or some of them, appear to assert a political influence. It is also clear that the culture wars of modern America show no sign of diminishing. If anything the reverse is true: moral conservatives continue to oppose secular liberals on a wide range of issues. Resistance to Evangelical ideas, however, is as likely to be found in the different currents of Christianity as it is in secularism as such. Indeed the failure of the Democrats in both the 2000 and 2004 presidential elections lay as much in their inability to take religion seriously as it did in their attempts to offer a secular alternative. Hence the despairing cry of Jim Wallis, whose book became the number one best seller on Amazon even before it was published. Its title *God's Politics: Why the Right Gets It Wrong and the Left Doesn't Get It* (2005) epitomizes the essential dilemma: many non-Republican Americans are looking for a religious rather than a secular alternative. It is this constituency, moreover, that the Democrats are so anxious to capture in 2008. That does not mean that secularists do not exist in America: they most certainly do, but they have a much harder time than their European counterparts in gaining a purchase in the population as a whole.

Two Outspoken Secularists

The difference can be illustrated by looking at two outspoken individuals.[9] The first is British—Richard Dawkins, a distinguished biologist at the University of Oxford; the second is American—Daniel Dennett, a philosopher from Tufts University in Massachusetts. Both could be described as "proselytizing" atheists.

Professor Dawkins, the holder of the Charles Simonyi Chair for the Public Understanding of Science, is widely admired for his pioneering work in evolutionary biology; his scientific views are well known both inside and outside the academy. He is a convinced Darwinian who combines the popularization of science with ever more trenchant attacks on religion. His latest book—*The God Delusion*—is concerned with the latter rather than the former. Published in 2006, it became very rapidly a best seller on both sides of the Atlantic. Both the book and its reception are central to the argument of this chapter: taken together they demonstrate a reaction in certain circles to the resurgence of religion in public discussion. Dawkins, incidentally, is genuinely perplexed by this phenomenon, noting in particular the persistence of religion in modern America—something that he cannot account for.

His response is robust to say the least. Both in the book itself and in television programs screened to coincide with publication,[10] the subtext (or in many places, the text) is unequivocal: the world would be a better place without religion. His argument, as a convinced and articulate atheist, deserves serious consideration; it is more than a rant against religion, though at times it comes perilously close to this. The approach, moreover, is deliberately polemical, in the sense that it often takes the form of a provocative statement, which is then corrected—by which time, of course, the damage is done. The following, frequently quoted passage is one such:

> The God of the Old Testament is arguably the most unpleasant character in all fiction: jealous and proud of it; a petty, unjust, unforgiving control freak; a vindictive, bloodthirsty ethnic cleanser; a misogynistic, homophobic, racist, infanticidal, genocidal, filicidal, pestilential, megalomaniacal, sadomasochistic, capriciously malevolent bully. (Dawkins 2006: 3)

A paragraph further on, Dawkins contrasts this portrait with the sentimental, largely nineteenth-century, image of a "gentle Jesus," pointing out that neither is complete or fully representative of Christian teaching, which must be countered in its entirety. Indeed the real question to be answered is the following: is there or is there not a superhuman intelligence that designed and created the universe, or is the latter simply the result of a long-term and continuing process of evolution? The title of Dawkins's text supplies the answer: the notion of God is a delusion. The contents, chapter by chapter, provide the evidence.

Most interesting for a sociologist of religion is Dawkins's attention to childhood. In his attempt to explain the persistence of religion in the modern world, Dawkins suggests that children have difficulty discriminating between the different pieces of wisdom that they hear from their parents. "Good" advice—to be careful crossing the road and so on—cannot be distinguished from what he considers much less good advice, that is the elements of religious doctrine that are passed from parent to child and so perpetuated. More than anything else, Dawkins takes exception to the idea of a "Catholic" child or a "Muslim" child—that, he feels, is an imposition on an individual who cannot yet decide for him or herself. Such labeling is effectively a curtailment of freedom.

His argument is intriguing—the more so given the number of recent studies that have emphasized not so much the perpetuation as the collapse in the religious tradition, most notably in Europe. Danièle Hervieu-Léger's *Religion as a Chain of Memory* (2000) offers an excellent example, and for two reasons. Not only does Hervieu-Léger argue that the chain of memory is close to breaking-point at least in the French case, but she takes that idea to its logical conclusion—one that might interest Professor Dawkins. What, precisely, might emerge when the memory of tradition as we know it can no longer be sustained? It may not be the well-informed, secular rationalism so desired by Dawkins, but a much more heterogeneous, fluctuating, and at times emotional, package of religious identities—half inside and half outside the historic churches. It is this not very reassuring situation that was described in Chapter 3.

The American case is rather different; here the handing-on process—for better or worse—is noticeably more intact. And it is in this much less questioning context that we must understand the work of Daniel Dennett, who with some justification has been called the "American Dawkins." Trained in philosophy rather than natural science, Dennett follows the same Darwinian line, in so far as he argues that humanity's affinity for religion is a by-product of evolution. Several chapters in his most recent book, *Breaking the Spell* (2006), describe how this process takes place. The tone of his writing, however, is noticeably different from Dawkins. Dennett's aim is to coax, rather than shock—to take his reader by the hand in order to ask questions that so far have been considered "off-limits" for many Americans. Such questions, for Dennett, go to the heart of the matter, in that they interrogate the widely held assumption that religion is a "good" thing, which enables people to live morally upright lives. Paragraph by paragraph, such assumptions are called into question. Minds, it follows, should be open rather than closed. And with the latter in mind, the position of children arises once again, with frequent reference to Dawkins's work. Less strident than his British equivalent, Dennett comes to a similar conclusion. He concludes: "If you have to hoodwink—or blindfold—your children to ensure that they confirm their faith when they are adults, your faith *ought* to go extinct" (2006: 328). The rights of the child to "freedom" are more important than the rights of the parent to pass on his or her belief system.

How then are these articulate and widely publicized atheists received in their respective communities? The answer is interesting. Professor Dawkins has a considerable following both in Britain and beyond—a fact that can be measured in audiences, television appearances, honorary doctorates, academic accolades, and so on. There are some, however— notably a section of the scientific community—who would prefer that Dawkins concentrated his energies on the popularization of science rather than the critique of religion. This, after all, is his primary role and a very necessary activity in a country in which the predilection of the young for studying science is diminishing rather than growing (see below). From this point of view, the continual sniping at religion is simply counterproductive. On the whole, however, Dawkins is recognized as a prominent intellectual, who is entitled both to his views on religion and to persuade others of their "delusions." He speaks to a significant minority—among them the 25 to 30 per cent of the British population, who will declare in an opinion poll that they have no belief in God. Such people, it is worth noting, will be predominantly male; they will also be clustered in certain professions, notably the media. Here, in short, is an accepted, but not necessarily typical minority who are disproportionately able to make their voices heard. Provoked by the reappearance of religion in public debate, both in Europe and beyond, they do precisely this.

In the United States, the proportions are different: those who believe in God constitute an overwhelming majority—over 90 per cent of the population. Atheists, it follows, are a somewhat beleaguered minority, one moreover which is unlikely to prosper in the political sphere. Only 37 per cent of the American population, it seems, would even contemplate voting for an American president who did not believe in God (Adler 2006). Also different are the arguments about religion in public life. Take, for example, the debate about creationism or intelligent design and its place in the public school system. A whole series of factors come together in this controversial issue, all of them illustrative of American life. They include very different understandings of "science," the place of these different interpretations in the education of young people, the proscribing of religion from the public school system, the politicization of the debate, and a specifically American decision-making process. For a British observer, one point stands out: it is right and proper, surely, for young people to discuss the origins of life and the possibility or otherwise that there might be a "creator" of some kind, but not—emphatically not—in a science class. In Britain, as indeed in most of Europe, such discussions would find their place in a lesson concerned with religious studies—an impossibility in the American system. Paradoxically, it is the absence of formal teaching in religion in the school system that has led to its reintroduction in the science class and the controversies that follow from this.[11] Interestingly, Dennett comes to the same conclusion. He is strongly in favor of teaching about religion, good points and bad, in the public schools of the United States (2006: 327).

A short post-script brings to a close this brief excursus into the teaching of religion in schools, which will be continued in Chapter 5. It concerns the educational choices of young people in Britain at the moment when they select certain subjects for specialized study. For most of the post-war period, it was widely assumed that science-based subjects would become ever more popular at the expense of religious education in its various forms. This would be the route to educational, economic, and social advancement. In the early years of the new century, such assumptions have been turned on their head—dramatically so. Both in the higher levels of the school system and at university entrance, the number of candidates seeking to do theology or religious studies is growing, if at times unevenly. Conversely, the numbers wanting to do science (particularly physics and chemistry) are falling—so much so that a significant number of science departments in public universities have been closed. Such closures are controversial, but it is no longer possible to maintain departments that are not attracting students. Why it should be so difficult to do this is not yet clear, but it is hardly evidence of secularization. The predilection for theology is equally complex. Anecdotal evidence suggests that it is driven by an interest in ethics and the philosophy of religion, rather than a return to biblical studies. Quite clearly more work is required in this field.

Signs of Change in Europe

There are other signs of change in Europe, in the sense that some European intellectuals are beginning to pay attention to religion. Or to put the same point in a different way, there are signs that the "secular neutrality" of the European Union is increasingly being called into question. Two

distinguished social scientists—José Casanova and Jürgen Habermas—
provide interesting illustrations of this shift.

Casanova has already been introduced as a critic of secularization
(pp. 15, 32–3). In his more recent writing, often focused specifically on
Europe, he approaches this topic in a rather different way. He begins by
articulating the following (secularist) paradox:

> In the name of freedom, individual autonomy, tolerance, and cultural pluralism,
> religious people—Christian, Jewish, and Muslim—are being asked to keep
> their religious beliefs, identities and norms "private" so that they do not disturb
> the project of a modern, secular, enlightened Europe. (2006: 66–7)

Such a statement quite clearly echoes the remarks made above concerning
the reassertions of religion in the public life of Europe and the difficulty
that European intellectuals have in dealing with these. It also builds on
Casanova's earlier thinking in his seminal book *Public Religions in the
Modern World* (1994), where he argues that religions both can and should
have a public role in the modern world, entering at every level into the
discursive space of civil society. Indeed, as his critique of the secularization
thesis develops throughout his work, Casanova poses increasingly sharp
questions. One such concerns the nature of secularization in Europe: is this
effectively a self-fulfilling prophecy? If it is, the secularization of western
Europe is likely to have more to do with the triumph of the knowledge
regime of secularism, than with structural processes of socio-economic
development (Casanova 2006: 84). It is for this reason, following Casanova,
that Europe should become, as rapidly as possible, post-secular. Only then
will it be possible to counter the secularist assumptions of many (if not all)
social and political commentators, who necessarily "turn religion into a
problem"—thus precluding the resolution of religion-related challenges in
a reasonable and pragmatic manner.

Habermas, perhaps the most prominent philosopher in modern Europe,
pursues a strikingly similar argument. This was the theme of a lecture
delivered on the occasion of the Holberg prize in 2005, and subsequently
expanded into a longer article (2006). The core of the lecture resides in the
following claim: secular citizens—Habermas insists—must learn, sooner
rather than later, to live in a post-secular society. In so doing, they will
be following the example of religious citizens, who have already come
to terms with the ethical expectations of democratic citizenship, in the
sense that they have adopted appropriate epistemic attitudes toward their
secular environment. So far secular citizens have not been expected to
make a similar effort—a situation which leads to the current "asymmetric
distribution of cognitive burdens," an imbalance which needs to be rectified
sooner rather than later (Habermas 2005).

The argument can be amplified as follows. Taking as his starting point the increasing significance of religious traditions and communities in much of the modern world (Berger 1999; Jenkins 2002), Habermas addresses the debate in terms of John Rawls's celebrated concept, the "public use of reason," using this to invite of secular citizens, including Europeans, "a self-reflective transcending of the secularist self-understanding of Modernity" (2006: 15)—an attitude that quite clearly goes beyond "mere tolerance" in that it necessarily engenders feelings of respect for the worldview of the religious person. Hence the need, not only for a growing reciprocity in the debate (see above), but for an additional question. Are religious issues simply to be regarded as relics of a pre-modern era, or is it the duty of the more secular citizen to overcome his or her narrowly secularist consciousness in order to engage with religion in terms of *"reasonably expected disagreement"* (2006: 15), assuming in other words a degree of rationality on both sides? The latter appears to be the case. Habermas's argument is challenging in every sense of the term and merits very careful reflection; it constitutes an interesting response to a changing global environment—one moreover in which the relative secularity of Europe is increasingly seen as an exceptional, rather than prototypical case.

More precisely, in the initial pages of Habermas's article, two closely linked ideas are introduced: on the one hand the increasing isolation of Europe from the rest of the world in terms of its religious configurations, and on the other the notion of "multiple modernities." It was exactly this combination that was developed in some detail in *Europe: The Exceptional Case* (Davie 2002). The starting point lies in reversing the "normal" question: instead of asking what Europe *is* in term of its religious existence, it asks what Europe is not. It is not (yet) a vibrant religious market such as that found in the United States; it is not a part of the world where Christianity is growing exponentially, very often in Pentecostal forms, as in the case in the southern hemisphere (Latin America, Sub-Saharan Africa, and the Pacific Rim); it is not a part of the world dominated by faiths other than Christian, but is increasingly penetrated by these; and it is not for the most part subject to the violence often associated with religion and religious difference in other parts of the globe—the more so if religion becomes entangled in political conflict. Hence the inevitable, if at times disturbing conclusion: that the patterns of religion in modern Europe, notably its relative secularity, might be an exceptional case in global terms.

Precisely that fact has become a central feature of the debate about multiple modernities, a theme already introduced, which must now be developed in more detail. The negative aspects of this idea are unequivocally set out in the following paragraph:

The notion of "multiple modernities" denotes a certain view of the contemporary world—indeed of the history and characteristics of the modern era—that goes against the views long prevalent in scholarly and general discourse. It goes against the view of the "classical" theories of modernization and of the convergence of industrial societies prevalent in the 1950s, and indeed against the classical sociological analyses of Marx, Durkheim, and (to a large extent) even of Weber, at least in one reading of his work. They all assumed, even if only implicitly, that the cultural program of modernity as it developed in modern Europe and the basic institutional constellations that emerged there would ultimately take over in all modernizing and modern societies; with the expansion of modernity, they would prevail throughout the world. (Eisenstadt 2000: 1)

Right from the start, therefore, the author—Shmuel Eisenstadt—challenges both the assumption that modernizing societies are convergent, and the notion that Europe (or indeed anywhere else) is the lead society in the modernizing process.

How then does the multiple-modernities approach develop from a positive point of view? In the introductory essay to an interesting set of comparative cases, Eisenstadt suggests that the best way to understand the modern world (in other words to grasp the history and nature of modernity) is to see this as "a story of continual constitution and reconstitution of a multiplicity of cultural programs" (2000: 2). A second point follows from this. These on-going reconstitutions do not drop from the sky; they emerge as the result of endless encounters on the part of both individuals and groups, all of whom engage in the creation and re-creation of both cultural and institutional formations, but within different economic and cultural contexts. Once this way of thinking is firmly in place it becomes easier to appreciate one of the fundamental paradoxes of Eisenstadt's writing: namely that to engage with the Western understanding of modernity, or even to oppose it, is as indisputably modern as to embrace it. It is equally clear that the form of modernity that has emerged in Europe is only one among many; it is not necessarily the global prototype.

Such a statement is crucial with respect to religion. It goes straight to the heart of the question that lies at the center of this book: is secularization intrinsic or extrinsic to the modernization process? In other words is Europe secular because it is modern (or at least more modern than other parts of the world), or is it secular because it is European, and has developed along a distinctive pathway unlikely to be repeated elsewhere? It also gathers up a number of threads already introduced, including the notion of a "lead society," and which one it is—Europe or the United States or neither? Equally significant is the fact that the dominant lines of thinking in modern social science—including thinking about religion—emerge from the European Enlightenment. And if the European case turns out to be exceptional rather than typical, where should we look for conceptual tools to understand better what is happening in the rest of the world? Hence the theoretical implications of these debates, not to mention their importance for policy. Both will be re-engaged in later chapters.[12]

At this stage, something rather more modest is required: that is to conclude this discussion of secular elites by looking in more detail at their relationship with the wider society, both in Europe and the United States.

High Culture and Popular Culture

An interesting "experiment" took place in London at Christmas 2006.[13] A chamber choir was sent to sing traditional carols in two rather different environments: the first—a respectable middle-class area, the second—a council estate, known for its social problems. The aim was "to test the appeal of doorstep carol-singing in modern Britain." The result was intriguing. The middle-class estate received the visitors courteously, but with a certain déjà vu. This choir was but one of many who had visited the area in the previous week or so, all of them asking for money (albeit for good causes). For the residents of the council estate, this was not the case: hence a degree of excitement as the presence of the choir made itself felt among the tower blocks. A specific invitation to sing to the older people provoked enthusiastic applause. Most interesting of all, however, was the response of a Muslim family on the estate—first in affirming that *Christian* carols were an entirely appropriate activity in a so-called Christian society, but also in the most generous donation of the evening. Indeed, the novelty was such that the choir were asked to sing loud enough for an uncle in Pakistan to hear them on the telephone!

An anecdote does not constitute social-scientific evidence. It does, however, give pause for thought regarding the wisdom of both elites and their policies regarding what has become known as multi-culturalism. The notion, for example, that specifically Christian festivals offend minorities from other faith communities is widespread—but it is rarely the view of the minorities themselves, who (equally rarely) are asked for their opinion. This could in fact be called a "battering-ram" approach to policy making: secular elites make use of other faith communities in order to further their own—frequently secular—points of view. They do not always consult before doing this. Hence, for example, the well-intentioned—if rather inept—idea of Birmingham City Council in the late 1990s to use the term Winterval rather than Christmas. The word "Christmas" was felt to be excluding of other faiths. Happily, the idea was abandoned after a couple of years, though the underlying debate re-emerges repeatedly (as indeed it does in the United States). The Christmas cards of politicians, for example, are carefully scrutinized for their political correctness. Their senders, however, find themselves between a rock and hard place: castigated by the chattering classes for specifically Christian greetings, they are taken to task by the popular press for the lack of them.

Rather more "scientific" are the data that emerged from the 2001 British Census, which for the first time in the history of the census in Britain contained a question about religion. Why this was so forms a study in its own right—admirably told by Francis (2003) and Weller (2004). In itself, it reveals a growing, though still controversial, awareness that religion should be seen as a public as well as private category in British life. Even more significant for the argument of this chapter is the fact that the driving force for the religious question in the census came from the other faith communities, notably the Muslims. In Britain, the Muslim population is diverse in terms of ethnicity and nationality. It follows that statistics based on either of these indicators disperse a purely religious identity and downplay for British Muslims what is for them the most important factor—their faith. British Muslims want to be known as Muslims in public as well as private life, in order that provision for their needs is met in these terms. Appropriate policies should be worked out on a secure statistical base (hence the demand for a specific question in the census), not on assumptions, estimates, or extrapolations from other variables.

Such a demand should be seen in a wider context. Very similar arguments, for example, can be found in a 2002 debate in the House of Lords on "Multi-Ethnicity and Multi-Culturalism," illustrating—in terms of a methodology—an interesting complementarity of sources (in this case, written text reinforcing the demand for statistical data). The following quotations exemplify the point perfectly; they are taken from a speech by Baroness Pola Manzila Uddin (2002), who—amongst many other honors—was the first Muslim in Britain to enter the House of Lords, and who remains the only Muslim woman in Parliament. The extracts speak for themselves:

> The almost total denial for decades of our identity based on our faith has been devastating psychologically, socially and culturally and its economic impact has been well demonstrated. For years Britain's 2 million or so Muslims ... have been totally bypassed even by the best-intentioned community and race relations initiatives because they have failed to take on board the fact that a major component of their identity is their faith.
>
> Such an identity demanded more than just the stereotypical and lazy imposition of simple cultural labels based on race categorisations. British Muslims, consisting of 56 nationalities and speaking more than 1,000 languages, have never been and shall never be happy about an existence and understanding that rarely goes beyond somosas, Bollywood and bhangra. (Uddin 2002: 1423)

Bearing these "stereotypical and lazy" impositions in mind, it was hardly surprising that the question on religion in the national census proved controversial. It also produced a typically British compromise: a different question emerged in England and Wales from that which was used in Scotland,[14] and both were optional rather than compulsory. Interestingly, the results from the two parts of the United Kingdom were somewhat different, revealing yet again that the formulation of a question has a powerful effect on how people respond, a point underlined by Voas and Bruce (2004).

How then should the findings of the census be interpreted? The Muslim community was rewarded in so far as its relatively modest presence was recognized as such. The same was true for the other religious minorities present in Britain, revealing their very different demographic profiles and their precise geographical locations. The Jewish community, for example, is significantly different in both respects from the more recently arrived religious minorities. Even more striking however was a point already mentioned in Chapter 3: that is the number of people in both populations, but especially in England and Wales (over 70 per cent), who declared themselves Christian –this was unexpectedly strong evidence of residual attachments. What though did the category "Christian" mean for those who ticked this box? Did this imply that the individuals concerned were not secular, or did it imply that they were not Muslim (or indeed another world faith), or did it mean something different again—a marker of national identity for example, as suggested by Voas and Bruce (2004)? It is at this point that more qualitative approaches to methodology become important; or at the very least some rather more detailed questions about religion addressed to a sample of those who answered "Christian" to the question about religious belonging. Until this is done, we can only speculate about the results.[15]

What conclusions can we draw from these data? First it is important to appreciate that Britain is not necessarily typical of Europe. In France, for example, a question about religion in the national census would be unthinkable. Indeed the lack of a reliable statistical base for the Muslim population in France is almost government policy: the whole point is not to identify, still less reify, the minority in question. And in France such policies—captured once again in the notion of *laïcité*—are, very largely, affirmed by the population as a whole. Broadly speaking, however, the European situation could be characterized by the existence of a secular elite, overlaying a largely indifferent, but "Christian" population. If provoked, the latter will still claim allegiance to the historic churches and expect these institutions to reciprocate at the time of need. Such residual attachments do not, however, imply a continuing knowledge of the

Christian narrative—quite the opposite in fact. The norm is widespread ignorance about religion, Christianity included—a state of affairs to which the label "everyday atheism" could be applied with some accuracy. Hence the bewildered response of the young man at the reception desk in the London hotel who really did not know what the Church of England was or where to find it (p. 9).

Something rather different exists in the United States. Here Berger is right to identify what Nancy Ammerman calls "golden-rule Christianity" as the majority position of most Americans. Golden-rule Christianity, moreover, is both more Christian and more active than its European counterpart, resisting on the one hand more extreme forms of Christianity, and on the other the unbelief of the secular elite—itself very much smaller, proportionally speaking, than its European equivalents. One point, however, is clear in both cases: that is, the importance of paying attention to the middle ground in sociological analysis. Small groups of opinion informers require careful study in their own right; that is clear. What really counts however is the capacity of these groups to gain a purchase in the wider population. It is this capacity, or the lack of it, that reveals a significant difference between Europe and the United States.

Concluding Remarks

Quite a bit of the previous section has focused on the British case, which can now be used to draw the threads of this chapter together. Here, without doubt, is a society pulled in two directions. As Himmelfarb makes abundantly clear, there is an affinity between the British and American Enlightenments—both are more pragmatic than the French example and both respect the common-sense doer rather more than the intellectual. Attitudes towards the state mirror these differences in the sense that Britain is moving steadily closer to the United States in terms of a state that regulates rather than provides. Britain, finally, acquired a relatively high degree of religious pluralism at an earlier stage than most Europeans, and learnt—though not always willingly—to tolerate religious differences at a group as well as individual level.

Britain, however, is firmly European in the sense that England and Scotland at least have a "state" church, in which the defining of territory at both national and local level is central—with all the advantages and disadvantages of this situation. The fact that the church is constitutionally different in each case does not effect the outcome[16]—which is a church that continues to operate as an effective public utility in time of need, but which is unable to move fast enough to accommodate the changes of late modernity in the sense of providing numerous and flexible options for an increasingly diverse population. The result is low levels of religious activity, very similar to those in most of northern Europe. In other words, the cultural affinities between Britain and the United States are countered by the institutional structures delivered by an essentially European past. It is these structures that provide the theme of the following chapter.

Notes

1   In France, in fact, the suppression of both Protestants and Protestantism had been particularly brutal, leading to widespread persecution, enforced conversions, and significant emigration among the Huguenot population.

2   A more detailed discussion of this approach can be found in Bouretz (2000).

3   In making this point, Bouretz is quite clearly following Gauchet (1985; 1999).

4   Interestingly, the British did not use the term "Enlightenment" at all, until well into the nineteenth century (Himmelfarb 2004: 9–11).

5   Agnesi was not alone in this respect. See Messbarger and Fidlen (2005) for further examples of women who excelled in the academy.

6   This essay on "the mystic heaven" (the full title of which is *Il cielo mistico, cioè contemplazione delle virtù, de' Misteri, e delle Eccellenze del Nostro Signore Gesù Cristo*), is Agnesi's contribution to an eighteenth-century mystical trend which emphasized personal love for Christ and a focus on his death and resurrection. See Mazzotti (2001: 673).

7   Details of TRES (a Network on Teaching Religion in a Multicultural European Society) can be found on the following website: http://www.student.teol.uu.se/tres/ (accessed 6 May 2008).

8   The reasons for East German secularity are complex; they include long-term historical developments in addition to the aggressive secularization policies of the communist government (McLeod 2000).

9   Dawkins and Dennett have been taken as examples. Militant atheism is a rapidly growing industry—see, for instance, the work of Sam Harris (2006; 2007) and Christopher Hitchens (2007). The sales figures for all these authors are high— something worthy of study in its own right. An excellent overview of this group and their motives can be found in Higgins (2007).

10 Two programs entitled "The Root of All Evil" were screened on British television's Channel 4 on 11 and 12 May 2006.

11 See for example Edward Larson's presentation to the Pew Forum on Religion in Public Life on "The Biology Wars: The Religion, Science and Education Controversy" December 5, 2005, and the debate that this provoked: http://pewforum.org/events/index.php (accessed 6 May 2008)

12 They are also developed in Davie (2007b).

13 *The Times*, 23 Dec. 2006, "The Knowledge" section: 27.

14 In Scotland, the question was much more detailed regarding different types of Christianity. See the official website of the census for further details: http://www.statistics.gov.uk/census2001/census2001.asp (accessed 6 May 2008).

15 An interesting start has been made in a recent doctoral thesis—see Day (2006).

16 An excellent source of information on church–state relationships in Europe, including the intricacies of the British case, can be found at: http://eurel. u-strasbg.fr/EN/index.php (accessed 6 May 2008).

Chapter 5

Variation Three: Institutional Carriers

Thus far we have discussed the different historical trajectories of religion in Europe and in the United States and the different understandings of the Enlightenment that underpin these stories. How, though, are these narratives both kept in place and passed on from one generation to another? What, in other words, are the institutional carriers—in addition to the churches themselves—that shape, influence, and perpetuate the patterns of religiousness in Europe and the United States respectively? The point has already been raised in passing in connection with Richard Dawkins's critique of religion; it is now time to develop it from a more positive point of view. Such an analysis builds naturally on to the approach set out in *Religion in Modern Europe* (Davie 2000), a book which envisaged religion in Europe as a form of collective memory, and then looked at the ways in which this is, or is not, perpetuated in the current situation. The results are complex to say the least. The debate, moreover, must include a normative dimension: what can or cannot be changed provokes heated discussion in any society, the more so when its core documents are under review. Hence a series of tensions that will resonate repeatedly in the pages that follow.

Clearly the state (or states in Europe) is the first place to look, a discussion that must include church–state relations. Indeed in many respects church–state relations constitute an umbrella under which the other institutions that are examined in this chapter find their place: these are the judiciary, education systems, and the providers of welfare, all of which display marked differences between Europe and the United States.[1] The judiciary, for example, has a very powerful role in determining the place of religion in the American public sphere. In Europe, it is primarily in national parliaments that such matters are negotiated, bearing in mind that the European Court of Human Rights is increasingly acting as a catalyst for change in this respect. Education is also different in the sense that religion is largely proscribed from the public school system in the United States, but not in Europe—with the important exception of France, where the education system quite clearly becomes the carrier of a secular ideology on behalf of the state. The provision of welfare, finally, reveals both ideological and institutional contrasts between the two cases, acknowledging once again that different European societies have chosen very different modes of delivery, underpinned by different political ideologies. Indeed it is at this point that post-Thatcherite Britain begins once again to lean towards the United States—not forgetting, however, the predilection of the British for their tax-funded National Health Service. As ever Britain finds itself facing in two directions at once.

Church–State Relations

An initial discussion of church–state relations took place in Chapter 3, beginning with de Tocqueville's observations about American society which have become classics in the field. The early parts of that chapter were concerned with the particular combinations that occur on each side of the Atlantic: that is, of religious vitality and the separation of church and state in the United States, alongside relative secularity and a history of church–state connections in Europe. Each of these had important consequences for sociological theory. Later sections revealed a more nuanced situation in which significant differences began to show—not least the established or concordat churches enjoying significant privileges at one end of the European spectrum as opposed to a strict separation of church and state at the other. The present chapter continues this discussion, concentrating initially on the American case.

Before doing so, however, one further observation is important—one, moreover, that introduces the first of the tensions that will underpin much of this material. That is the need to keep separate, at least for analytical purposes, two overlapping phenomena: on the one hand the constitutional apparatus that exists in each country, and on the other the continuing chain of political events that takes place within this. In practice, of course, each reinforces the other: the constitution frames the ways in which political business is conducted; political decisions confirm the constitution. "Real life" however, is inherently messy, taking the edge off constitutional sharpness—allowing, amongst other things, a degree of contradiction between the two. What is separate in the constitution may not be quite so clear in the cut and thrust of everyday life (see below). Every now and again, however, low-level contradictions turn into sharper tensions, to the point when religious and political pressures combine to force a change in the constitutional provision—one such occurred in France in 1905, the significance of which has already been underlined. Much more benignly, Sweden turned its state church into a free folk church in 2000, on the grounds that a privileged state church was no longer appropriate in an increasingly plural society. Norway is very likely to follow suit a generation or so later.

In the American case, "real life" most certainly plays its part; so too does the notion of "civil religion" described in Chapter 3. The discussion of the United States must begin, however, with the Constitution itself— more precisely with the two clauses that are central to religion in American society: that is the "establishment clause" and the "free exercise clause" of the First Amendment to the Constitution.[2] But here too, there is an immediate and widely recognized difficulty—each of these clauses pushed to the limit has the potential to interfere with the other. Allowing unlimited free exercise of religion in a public institution, for example, will sooner or later impinge on establishment. Quite apart from this, the free exercise clause grants certain protections to religion that other aspects of life do not enjoy through explicit reference in the Constitution; conversely, the establishment clause sets limits on religion which are not set for other aspects of life. As one analyst remarks, regarding each clause respectively: "There is no parallel constitutional protection for free exercise of tourism, boating, hiking, beer drinking, or environmentalism ... [and] there are no parallel clauses preventing the establishment of science, philosophy, or speech" (Pepper 1982: 293–4).

Unsurprisingly, these tensions are not only recognized, but have provoked extensive debates about the intentions of the drafters of the American Constitution. Manion, to give but one example, maintains that the fact that the establishment clause comes first in the text of the First Amendment, indicates a prioritization of this clause over the one that follows (2002: 318–19). Monsma (2000), on the other hand, argues against the notion that a tension between the two clauses was somehow intended by the framers of this document. He also rejects the theory that such a tension is in some way necessary for the balancing of each clause against the other—an interpretation, he feels, that would undermine the importance of each clause taken separately.

But quite apart from the niceties of academic debate, what happens in practice is in itself evidence of the drafters' intentions. It is the American judiciary (and mainly the Supreme Court)—as the interpreter of the Constitution—that decides where the balance between the two clauses should lie, doing this on a case by case basis. Accordingly, the balance is in a constant state of flux and depends to a considerable extent on the members of the Supreme Court at any one time. It is for this reason that the appointment of justices is so crucial—such appointments become not only controversial but highly politicized. The two most recent, made by George W. Bush, exemplify the point perfectly. Both John Roberts (appointed 2005) and Samuel Alito (appointed 2006) were subject to considerable public scrutiny regarding their views of the place of religion in American society, and at two levels: their personal opinions were carefully noted, so also was the overall balance of opinion in the Supreme Court that would result from their appointments. Both aspects continue to resonate.

That is one side of the picture. Another can be found in the propensity, or otherwise, of American citizens to take particular cases to court and to pursue these to the Supreme Court level. These inclinations change over time. For example, during the 1960s—a time of many societal changes, protests, and upheavals, when "traditional values" came under sustained attack—the Supreme Court addressed a number of popular religious practices in public schools. These include the landmark *Engel v. Vitale* (1962) case challenging the mandatory recitation of a prayer in New York public schools; *Chamberlin v. Public Instruction Board* (1964) on Bible readings and prayer recitations in Florida public schools; and *Epperson v. Arkansas* (1968) which challenged the teaching of evolution in public schools or universities. Interestingly, in each case the religion-oriented practices were deemed unconstitutional (Manion 2002: 321).

Thus—and this is the crucial point—fundamental decisions which shape the place of religion vis-à-vis the American public sphere are contingent on a number of factors: on individual judges, on partisan interests in the sense that appointments to the Supreme Court are made by the President, and finally on the "spirit of the times." These delicate and continually shifting equations are, however, but one of several factors to note regarding church–state relations in the United States. Additional complexities derive from the federal system—in the sense that federalism has resulted in different interpretations of the "religion clauses" throughout America. It is only when a court case reaches the Supreme Court, through a long and arduous process, that a ruling related to religion is to apply at the national level. But even then, its implementation across the country cannot be taken for granted.

This is even more the case when the ruling itself is ambiguous. For example, *Everson v. Board of Education* (1947) is considered a seminal case in establishment clause law, in which Jefferson's "wall of separation" was (emotively) evoked in the ruling emphasizing the strict separation between church and state. In the same case, however, the court ruled in favor of the state's allowing public funds to be used for the transporting of students to and from private (in this case, mainly Catholic) schools. Separationist rhetoric, in other words, accompanied what was in fact an accommodationist ruling. To a large extent the same ambiguity underlies the multiple federal approaches to state provision of vouchers for redemption at religious schools. For example, Milwaukee (Wisconsin),

Cleveland (Ohio), and the states of Florida and Colorado have voucher programs, while tax credits to parents of religious-school students are offered in other states.[3]

A third, related, and rather more down-to-earth feature cannot be avoided in this discussion—that is the disproportionate attention given to religion-related matters which involve questions of money. Unsurprisingly, the allocation of resources raises more hackles than constitutional interpretation per se, a fact with direct consequence for the interpretation of the Constitution. *De facto*, it means that there are more discussions, debates and court cases concerning the establishment clause than the free exercise clause, given that the former is much more likely than the latter to involve public policy decisions regarding subsidies and other tangible benefits such as school choice vouchers, tax benefits, student assistance programs, and so on.

Recent decisions exemplify this point; they also illustrate the independent nature of Supreme Court decisions. During the years of the George W. Bush administration, for instance, a number of church–state cases have been settled in favor of greater state sponsorship of religious activities. However, in 2004, the Supreme Court significantly departed from this trend in the *Locke v. Davey* ruling. Here the court upheld the right of Washington state to rescind a student's scholarship when the latter stated his intention to use it for pastoral studies: the state constitution prevents public payments for the training of clergy. Justice Antonin Scalia's dissenting opinion pointed to "the indignity of being singled out for special burdens on the basis of one's calling," while Chief Justice William H. Rehnquist, writing the majority opinion, supported the state's right not to fund a distinct category of instruction and argued that "training someone to lead a congregation is an essentially religious endeavor." The case is significant because a ruling in the student's favour would have made it easier to enforce state provision of vouchers for religious schools.[4] It would also have complemented the faith-based initiatives introduced by the post-2001 Bush administration (see below).

The more you look, in fact, the more complex the system becomes. In many ways this is to be expected, but even if all the above factors are taken into account, the outside observer may still be puzzled by the apparent contradictions in the American system. Why, for example, is public prayer not allowed in public schools, yet the United States Congress employs chaplains to lead its own daily prayers? How, moreover, "can a system that proclaims 'In God We Trust' as its national motto, invokes the name of God in its pledge of allegiance, observes a national day of prayer, and sanctions government-paid legislative chaplains be said to have a commitment to the separation of church and state?" (Davis 2001:6). The key to understanding this contradiction lies in a point already made: that is the distinction between institutional separation on the one hand, and the much more complex realities of everyday living on the other. Separation is observed mostly through judicial decisions that limit religious activity in the public schools. At the same time, the close links between religion and politics are almost palpable in modern America, particularly during national elections. This is the way the United States works.

A strict separation of church and state can also be found in parts of Europe, most notably in France. The French version of church–state separation is, however, fundamentally different from that found in the United States. An anecdote makes this abundantly clear. In his presentation of the Supreme Court majority decision on prayer in American public schools, one Supreme Court Justice explained that "religion is too personal, too sacred, too holy, to permit its 'unhallowed perversion' by a civil magistrate" (Justice Hugo Black, cited in Davis 2003a: 430).[5] In other words religion in the United States needs protecting from the state. In France, precisely the reverse is the case: the state needs protecting from religion—a reflex that reveals time and time again the almost irrational fear of the French for seriously held religious belief, especially when this appears in unexpected guises.

The point can be exemplified many times over. A particularly pertinent illustration can be found in the debate surrounding sects or new religious movements in France—the term "sect," in fact, is the most usual in France, in which the pejorative overtone is deliberate. The following quotation goes straight to the heart of the matter. It is taken from Danièle Hervieu-Léger's analysis of the French attitude to sects in the early years of the twenty-first century.[6] The "system" referred to in the first sentence evokes the constitutional provisions put in place at the time of the separation of church and state in France, a crucially important episode in French history already referred to more than once:

> The system topples when the mesh of the confessional net is strained by the multiplication of groups and movements claiming religious status and demanding the benefits of a freedom taken for granted in democratic societies. In reaction to the anarchic proliferation of self-proclaimed and extradenominational religious groups, *laïcité's* deep-rooted suspicion that religious alienation poses a constant threat to freedom is tending to resurface. (Hervieu-Léger 2001b: 254)

A whole range of factors come together in these sentences: the frameworks (both legal and conceptual) set in place in France in 1905, the quintessentially French notion of *laïcité*, the transformation of the religious scene in the late twentieth century, and the clearly normative reactions of French officialdom and the French public to these changes. Indeed it is these reactions that reveal the issues at stake in this debate: first—what can and cannot count as religion and who should decide; and second—a widespread and very French belief that religion as such might be a threat to freedom. The size of the questions are, it seems, inversely related to the size of the movements in question; equally striking are the contrasts with the United States.

Both questions and contrasts will be readdressed in Chapter 6 with reference to the newly arrived and much larger religious minorities, notably Islam. Here, a rather different point requires attention. That is the fundamental ambiguity in the French case, which mirrors surprisingly closely the tensions between the two clauses of the American Constitution. In declaring itself *laïque*—which, at its simplest, means the absence of religion from the public sphere—the French state has to decide how to apply this principle. More precisely it has to decide whether the state should simply stay out of religious debates altogether (that is one interpretation of "absence"), or whether it is the role of the state to create *laïque* citizens in a more active or positive sense. Is it the role of the state, for example, to educate citizens about religion, including its dangers, and—if so—how might this be done? It is at this point that the links between the state and the professional corps of teachers become so crucial in the French case, a relationship to be considered in some detail below.

At a more philosophical level, it is interesting to note two parallel and rather different understandings of *laïcité*. Jean Baubérot—the distinguished holder of the chair in the history and sociology of *laïcité* at the Ecole Pratique des Hautes Etudes in Paris[7]—paid close attention to these contrasts in a decade dominated in France by the increasingly problematic *affaire du foulard*. On the one hand can be found what amounts to an exclusive version of *laïcité*—one that reveals an anti-religious connotation which can still be felt. On the other lies a more inclusive and flexible approach, which represents an ongoing effort to interrogate or redefine *laïcité* in light of changing circumstances. Both, moreover, existed from the outset in the sense that, taken together, they express a by now familiar tension between freedom of conscience (claimed by religious actors of all kinds) and freedom of thought (claimed, in the French case, by the teaching establishment); if pushed to the extreme, the two are incompatible. How then are these tensions to be worked out in the circumstances of the twenty-first century?

The Judiciary

Before answering this question, it is important to return to the American case. Up to now we have paid attention to the judiciary in so far as the Supreme Court interprets the constitutional issues that have to do with the two vital clauses of the First Amendment. The judiciary, however, merits more detailed attention in that it is an institution with considerable influence over many different aspects of religion in the United States. (So far local and national courts do not play a comparable role in Europe, though things may change as pan-European institutions begin to affirm their role.) Indeed in the American context, it could almost be said that the judiciary occupies an "umbrella position," alongside the constitution as such, in that it acts as a space through which other religion-related domains (education and healthcare for example) are negotiated. Two landmark judicial issues will be taken as examples—one from each domain: first the constitutionality of the recitation of the Pledge of Allegiance in public schools, and secondly the right of a woman to have an abortion.

The "Pledge of Allegiance narrative" becomes in fact a useful prism through which to address a number of important points regarding the American judiciary. The first of these is the time-lag effect in the process as a whole. The pledge was drafted in 1892, without the words "under God," which were added in 1954 (in the cold war context). It was not until 2003, however, that its daily recitation in public schools was challenged by a California court of federal appeals as a violation of the establishment clause, on the grounds that the words "under God" revealed a religious orientation in what was meant to be a public—that is, non-religious— text.[8] Significantly, the time-lag has to do with the factors outlined in the previous section: they include the social context at a given moment in history when such a case may arise, the particular justices instated during the given period, and the different levels of the judiciary (local, state, and national), all of which had an effect on how the issue of the pledge's constitutionality was handled.

A further, rather more complex, ingredient concerns the significance of religion in American society more generally. Although the California court ruling against the constitutionality of reciting the pledge in public schools is deemed by most experts as correct (more specifically, as satisfactorily fulfilling the "Lemon test" of establishment clause violations),[9] a strong backlash—within both the Senate and the House of Representatives—was waged against the ruling. Specifically, the notion that the reciting of the pledge in schools could be considered unconstitutional was thought by the President (George W. Bush) to be "ridiculous and inconsistent with the traditions and history of America" (Davis 2003b: 657). Significant sections of the American population would agree with him. Who then should prevail?

The California judge charged with writing the opinion makes the essential point: "We may not—we must not—allow public sentiment or outcry to guide our decisions" (Davis 2003b: 657–8). In other words, constitutionality is more important than public sentiments in deciding violations of the establishment clause. Strict constitutionality however, was difficult to maintain in the political context in which this case rose to public attention (i.e. not long after 9/11). The next step, in fact, is revealing. The case reached the Supreme Court in 2004, but the constitutionality of the recitation in schools (concerning the words "under God") was not addressed. Instead, the court rejected the claim of the parent who raised the case in California, on the grounds that he "lacked standing" to do this, given that he was not the custodial parent. (He was, in fact, in a legal battle with the mother of the child over custody rights.) The crucial question—the continuing tension between constitutionality and everyday opinion—was thus avoided, but it cannot be sidelined for long. Sooner or later it will assert itself: how can strict separation be maintained alongside the evident presence of religion at every level of American society, formal as well as informal? The debate, no doubt, will continue.

A rather different set of issues arise in cases that involve a moral as well as a legal dimension. Here the American judiciary acts in some senses as a public debating chamber—with a nation-wide audience—for difficult questions. One such concerns the legality of abortion, a topic that touches the core of the belief systems of many faith communities. So explosive is this issue, in fact, that the Supreme Court has expressly avoided addressing it under the First Amendment "religion clauses," and has instead handled the question of abortion as a "right to privacy" or "personal liberties" assured under the Fourteenth rather than the First Amendment. To be precise, the landmark case *Roe v. Wade* formally protects the personal right of a woman to have an abortion before "viability" (i.e. before the foetus could survive outside the womb); it says nothing of religious beliefs, theologies, creation, and so on (Simmons 2000: 74).

Whatever the constitutional details, few Supreme Court cases have drawn as much attention as *Roe v. Wade*, and even now, some forty years after the ruling, American society is still divided over this case. Many groups and individuals continue to struggle against it—whether through the waging of other court cases relating to abortion, or through public protests at abortion clinics. The latter in fact brought about a second court case: *Bray v. Alexandrian Women's Health Clinic* (1993). *Bray* is considered to be a major setback for the *Roe* supporters, in its upholding of the right of pro-lifers to protest outside abortion clinics. Clearly, this remains an open subject both for American society and for the American judiciary. The former, moreover, continues to look to the latter in its efforts to resolve this highly contentious issue. It is for this reason that those nominated as members of the Supreme Court are subject to such intense scrutiny regarding their views on abortion.[10] A comparable situation is difficult to imagine in Europe, which does not mean simply that Europeans "don't care" about this issue. Many of them do, but they go about resolving it in rather different ways.

The nearest parallel in Europe to the American Supreme Court—the European Court of Human Rights (ECtHR)—works differently. For a start, rather like most other aspects of pan-Europeanism, it does not have a broad audience.[11] There is, in consequence, no public space in Europe comparable to the United States Supreme Court in which matters related to religion might be handled. It seems, however, that the ECtHR might be moving in that direction. The reasons are clear enough: increasing public attention is being paid to religious matters in Europe, as similar issues present themselves in different European countries. Common themes underpin these episodes in the sense that almost all of them concern the understanding and application of religious freedoms in a context where expressions of religion are becoming increasingly diverse.

At this point, yet another tension begins to emerge if we turn our attention to the European Union: this time between two of the European Union's foundational principles when it comes to matters related to religion – these are the principle of subsidiarity and the principle of pluralism (Fokas 2008). On the one hand, and with respect to national specificity, the principle of subsidiarity requires that matters that can be effectively addressed at the national level should be so addressed, without European Union intervention. On the other, the European Union claims at one and the same time to be both religiously and philosophically neutral, and devoted to the principle of pluralism. Thus it aims to influence member states in such a way as to create environments conducive to religious diversity. These two interests (subsidiarity and pluralism), however, are likely to come into conflict in particular cases. This is clearly so when the handling of religious matters in certain member states impedes the flourishing of pluralism. As a result, the Union is likely to communicate mixed signals to member states on issues to do with religion.

An excellent example of mixed signals can be found in conflicting interpretations of Article 9 (on religious freedom) of the European Convention on Human Rights (ECHR). It is nicely captured in an article in *The Economist* aptly entitled "Welcome to the confused and the confusing world of European Islam" published in 2005. The following extract reveals the problem:

A Danish supermarket fires a cashier for wearing a headscarf on the grounds that it might get stuck in the till. The German state of Baden-Württemberg prohibits the wearing of headscarves by teachers, not students. France bans the garment altogether from state schools, citing Article 9 of the European Convention on Human Rights. A British court cites the same article to uphold a schoolgirl's right to wear the much bulkier covering knows as a jilbab.

The problem, moreover, is likely to get worse rather than better. In recent years, the interpretation of Article 9 has been rendered even more complicated in the face of challenges related to Article 10, which protects the freedom of speech. Two episodes in particular brought the tension between these two articles to a climax in controversies which began in Europe but sent shock waves through the whole world: first, the printing in the Danish *Jyllands-Posten* (in the autumn of 2005), and subsequent reprintings elsewhere, of cartoons of Mohammed, and second the remarks made about Islam by Pope Benedict XVI in his speech in Regensburg (in September 2006). The sharp backlash amongst many Muslims in each case provoked intense debates in Europe about where the line should be drawn between freedom of religion and freedom of speech. Such debates are not easily resolved.

Education Systems

The examples drawn to our attention in the quotation from the *The Economist* in the previous section are indicative of a notable similarity between Europe and the United States: educational institutions serve as a major battlefield for the negotiation of religious matters. This is hardly surprising given the desire of key protagonists to win the hearts and minds of young people. The battle, however, is differently engaged in each case. In Europe, the historic churches have played a major part in the education of children—and in many parts of the continent, they still do. This can be seen in two rather different ways: in the management and ownership of significant numbers of schools, and in the manner in which religious education as such is handled in the public school systems of different European societies. Both will be discussed in this section.

Before expanding on these examples, however, it is important to acknowledge the cases where religion is conspicuous by its absence from schools—that is, in the United States and in France. In the former, the teaching of religion is officially proscribed from the school system—a fact with important implications for the curriculum, some of which were explored in the previous chapter. Here a different point is underlined: it concerns the "logic" of the American argument. In a substantially churchgoing country, the teaching of or about religion remains an entirely laudable activity—that much is clear. It is not, however, the responsibility of either the state or the public school system to ensure that such teaching takes place. Quite the reverse in fact. Indeed for these essentially public institutions to intrude into this area would be seen by many Americans as threatening to both the independence and the integrity of religion.

Two important issues follow from this. The first relates to what might be called alternative provision, including on the one hand private schools (many of which are firmly religious), and on the other the right of parents to home-school their children—something far more common in the United States than in Europe. Predictably, those who do not feel happy about sending their children to public schools (for whatever reason) are particularly vigilant in this respect, revealing—though not always in the same way—an underlying theme: religion must be shielded from outside interference. Some groups, for example, express this by ensuring state protection for private religious establishments; others are much more wary—seeing in state support of whatever kind (including student finance), a necessarily corrupting influence. The second issue is somewhat different: it concerns the general running of an educational institution, à propos of which a whole series of constitutional debates assert themselves. These include the prohibition of prayer in schools, including tricky decisions as to whether this should or should not be extended to moments of silence, and the mandatory recitation of the Pledge of Allegiance already considered. The vexed question of religious displays on public property—for example the display of the Ten Commandments on the Colorado state capitol grounds—is not strictly an educational issue, but raises similar questions on which separationists take one view, accommodationists quite another. Each group, moreover, appeals to the constitution to justify its position in a debate that ebbs and flows over time, but never recedes altogether.

In France, American priorities are largely reversed: the school system, like the French state, must be protected from religion.[12] Historically, this meant freeing the system from the influence of the Catholic Church, a battle that raged throughout the nineteenth century, culminating in the separation of church and school in 1882—that is, some twenty years before the definitive separation of church and state. The establishment of a strictly secular school system in which there is no place for religion in the curriculum or for religious personnel in teaching or management was the result. The school system in fact became an essential tool in the building of the French nation: in the transmission of the French language (a story in its own right) and in the instilling in the population of a distinctive value system. Absolutely central to this value system is the notion of *laïcité*, already described. In this sense Berger is entirely correct to underline the role of education in the development of secularity in the French case. French schools, more specifically French school teachers, have become the disseminators of a value-system, which in its strong forms rigorously opposes religion (initially that meant the Catholic Church), and in its weaker forms ensures that religion is, once and for all, relegated to the private sphere.

That, however, is not the whole story. First there are important exceptions to the general rule. This is not the place to explore the intricacies of the French system, with its regional specificities; it is however important to recognize that, even in France, private (mostly Catholic) schools not only exist, but receive public funding. The French have very clear ideas on this issue, and if necessary will take to the streets to express them. Even more significant for the argument of this chapter, however, is the recent rethinking about the place of religion in the school curriculum—the more so if we take into account the reasons for this reappraisal. These reside in a growing awareness that students educated in France are inadequately prepared for modern living, in as much as the latter necessarily entails encounters with religion. Such unpreparedness resonates in a wide variety of fields—in the teaching of art and literature, in the comprehension of politico-religious conflicts in the modern world, and in the need to appreciate the needs and aspirations of the sizeable Muslim community currently living in France. Bit by bit the system has begun to change as "religious facts" are reintroduced into different parts of the teaching curriculum. Willaime (2007) gives a clear account of this continually evolving story. These features tend, however, to pale into insignificance, when placed against the episode that will be described in more detail in the following chapter: that is the absolute ban on religious symbols in the French public school system imposed in 2004. Provoked by the *affaire du foulard*, this ban symbolizes the continuing difficulties of the French government when faced with the presence of religion in public life.

So much for the French case. In the rest of Europe, Berger's claim that the education system is the primary channel of either secularity or secularism is more difficult to sustain. Indeed the reverse may well be true. It is equally possible to argue that the school system remains an important carrier of religious memory, especially amongst younger generations. If young people in Europe have any knowledge of religion at all, whether their own or anyone else's, they are likely to have acquired this in school. The two ways in which this process takes place were set out at the beginning of this section. It is now time to engage each of these in turn.

The first concerns the continuing place for the churches in the ownership and management of European schools. Historically the position is clear: for much of European history, education remained largely under the influence of the dominant church. The process of modernization, however, exacted its price: as the state asserted its influence over education (as it did over health and welfare), religious institutions progressively lost control. As we saw in Chapter 3, this shift—essentially a transfer of power—denotes a pivotal change in European societies. The process, however, was gradual and, even now, is by no means complete; indeed in the majority of European societies, the historic churches have retained a significant stake in the delivery of education. The story has been told many times over (see Davie 2000) and is not the primary focus of this chapter. Here the argument turns on a related but distinct question. It is this: if the historic churches of Europe have retained the ownership and control of a significant proportion of schools in any given society, should a similar privilege be extended to the faith communities that have arrived in Europe much more recently? Unsurprisingly, a particular area of controversy has developed with respect to Muslim schools: should they or should they not be supported with public money?

Europe offers a kaleidoscope of answers to these questions. The following should be considered as indicative rather than exhaustive illustrations. The British case is the best known and is often cited.[13] The Dutch example, however, is equally interesting, particularly in that it tells us a great deal about "Dutchness." The system itself dates back to the 1917 "Pacification Act," which ended a long-running political dispute about the funding of education in the Netherlands. The act established the "pillarization" of the education system—whereby each religious group (at the time, Protestants and Roman Catholics) could run its own schools. Even more pertinently, denominational schools have received the same financial support as state schools, a system gradually extended to other faiths. Currently, Islamic schools make up less than 1 per cent of Dutch schools, a hardly significant figure. Their existence, however, constitutes the tip of a very much larger iceberg. Since 9/11, and even more so since the murder of Theo van Gogh in Amsterdam, the Dutch have looked again at their system. Multiculturalism has been questioned; so too has the system that sustains it. Seen in this light the "Pacification Act" becomes not so much the solution, as the root of a deep-seated problem in Dutch society—a problem that manifests itself in the lack of encounter and dialogue, much less cohesion, between the different groups of peoples now living in this densely populated corner of Europe (ter Avest et al. 2007).

In Greece, a very different situation pertains. Here state-funded schools belonging to other faith communities operate only in Thrace (in northern Greece), where there are two Koranic schools serving a very specific group of Muslims. Both the presence of this community, and its subsequent educational rights, are dictated by the Lausanne Treaty of 1923, which followed the population exchange between Greece and Turkey after the 1919–22 Greco-Turkish War. And while the Dutch system of funding was systematically extended to include an increasing number of religious groups, the Greek concession was not—emphatically not. It remains confined to a particular community, guaranteed only in exchange for similar rights for the Greek minority in Istanbul. Each system, in fact, reflects wider national struggles, both internal and external. In order to be fully understood, each must be set in its own historical context.

The second area of interest relates specifically to the teaching of religion in the school systems of Europe—a necessarily complex topic which contains within it many different and contradictory elements, best expressed as a series of questions. For example: is religious education which is primarily confessional in nature still acceptable in twenty-first century Europe? If so, should it be mandatory for all children? Who, moreover, should decide the exceptions, and what provision should be made for these students? If not, who—in a modern and increasingly plural society—should decide the content of the non-confessional religious education syllabus? Who should teach it? How should these people be trained, by whom, and which textbooks should they use? Such questions could continue almost indefinitely. Answers, however, are difficult to come by and, quite clearly, vary across Europe. In the north, for example, most school systems have adopted a non-confessional curriculum that informs rather than indoctrinates. This is very much less so in, say, Greece or Italy, where the dominant churches still hold sway. The questions, moreover, must be asked repeatedly. Most Europeans would agree that students can be withdrawn from classes that are clearly confessional. Much less clear is the continuation of that privilege when confessional teaching has been replaced by something else. In England and Wales, for example, the exemption clause has been maintained, even after the teaching of religious education has become non-confessional in nature. Old habits die hard in this respect.

What in fact emerges is a bewildering variety of policies on religious education through which it is difficult to pick a clear path. One commentator suggests the following categorizations. The legal status of religious education, whether confessional or not, in the pre-2004 European Union is as follows: it is mandatory in Greece, Sweden, Austria, and Finland; it is mandatory but with request of exemption in Germany, Luxembourg, and the United Kingdom; it is mandatory for the educational centers but optional for students in Spain and Portugal; and is available by request upon enrolment in Belgium, Holland, Ireland, and Italy (Gomez-Quintero 2004: 562). Not everyone would agree with the details of this listing, nor is it sufficiently nuanced (for example, exemption is possible in Greece but only for the non-Orthodox), but it gives an idea of what is, or is not, available in different European societies. As with the question of Muslim schools, the questions are all the more difficult in so far as national, as well as religious, identities are often at stake.

The following examples illustrate three very different ways of dealing with the problem. The first two introduce new cases, the third returns to the Greek situation. Once again, each reveals a quite distinct historical context. In Germany, for example, the experience of World War II was and remains paramount. With this in mind, it was necessary to strike a careful balance regarding the legal status of religious education— one which allowed the state to remain open to religion in general, but without controlling the syllabus as such. The solution, firmly embedded in the post-war constitution, is instructive. It gave to the two established churches (one Catholic and one Protestant) a considerable responsibility: that of developing, independently, the content of religious education in German schools (Knauth 2007: 244–5). This freedom from state control was deemed a crucial aspect of the newly developing German nation. How it should be pursued in a more religiously diverse society poses new and interesting questions. Equally complex are the implications of German unification, given the marked secularity of eastern Europe in which an entirely different system obtained.

In Norway, the Education Act of 2000 reflects a very different situation. Primary and lower-secondary education exist "to give pupils a Christian and moral upbringing, to develop their mental and physical abilities, and to give them good general knowledge so that they may become useful and independent human beings at home and in society" (Skeie 2007: 229). Even more precisely, the General Core Curriculum (in place since 1993) includes the following goal: "familiarity with our Christian and humanist heritage—and knowledge of and respect for other religions and faiths" (Skeie 2007: 229). The two last are recognized as "dual aims" in Norwegian education, the tension between which must be reconciled. In Norway, as elsewhere, such reconciliations (if achieved at all) very often take the form of policy recommendations. One such recommendation, located in a recent Norwegian white paper, was both practical and symbolic in suggesting that religious education be entitled "identity and dialogue": the "identity" aspect recognizes the importance of belonging to a tradition, and the "dialogue" aspect emphasizes the importance of communication between people from different traditions (Skeie 2007: 234). What emerges, in other words, is a quintessentially Norwegian solution to the "problem" at hand.[14]

A quintessentially Greek non-solution to the same problem is expressed somewhat differently, this time through a series of disagreements relating to church–state policies regarding religious education. In Greece, the state has sought to weaken, bit by bit, the church's hold over religious education in public schools, which until very recently, was almost entirely Orthodox. Progress, however, is slow. Exemption is now possible for non-Orthodox students, but the shift from confessional religious education to a more "history of religions" approach is much more challenging. As in Norway, the stated purpose of various levels of religious education—is indicative of wider aspirations—revealing, in the Greek case, the indissoluble links between religious and national identity. At primary and secondary levels, for example, religious education exists to "help the students possess faith towards the fatherland and towards the genuine elements of the Orthodox Christian tradition." At tertiary level, the program includes the student's "awareness of the deeper importance of the Orthodox Christian ethos" (Dimitropoulos 2001: 146). In other words, in education—as in everything else—the disentangling of religious and national identity in Greece is particularly difficult to achieve.

It is now possible to draw a number of threads together. European societies are all engaged in a similar process: how to bring their educational policies into line with the changing nature of societies of which they are part—that is, societies which combine declining levels of religiousness overall with the growing presence of religious minorities. The crucial point to grasp is that each of these societies does this within a distinctive, historically determined framework of church–state relationships and educational provision, bearing in mind that the two are closely related. Some European nations are clearly more advanced in this process than others, and some appear to be more successful than others, though none have found it easy.

The Provision of Welfare

It is now time to consider our final example: the contrasts between the United States and Europe in both the conception and practice of welfare, and the relevance of these differences for religious activity. At first glance, the differences are striking. In Europe, it is axiomatic (almost) that the state should take responsibility for the basic needs of the population. It is this assumption, moreover, that underpins the "welfare state"—an essentially positive term strongly associated with the notion of solidarity. The welfare state becomes thereby a significant aspect of European heritage, both paralleling and, in many respects, continuing the traditional role of the majority church. In America, every one of these assumptions is different. For a start, there is no state church (that point is already clear); there is also no state in the sense that this is understood in Europe—a fact which has considerable implications for everything that follows. The state which is responsible for welfare in Europe is, in itself, a European construction. The word "welfare," finally, has very different connotations. What is to be welcomed in Europe, becomes all too often in the United States (at least in popular parlance) a waste of tax payers hard-earned money—it simply encourages the work shy.

With this in mind, it is hardly surprising that social policy specialists see the welfare provision of the two societies as the outworking of contrasting political philosophies: of European collectivism (or egalitarianism) on the one hand, and of American individualism (or free enterprise) on the other. Equally varied are the value judgments that follow. Looked at from Europe, for instance, the American picture is distinctly unflattering. Its welfare state (the existence of which many will not even acknowledge) is not only smaller than most European equivalents, but "less inclusive, less generous, and more fragmented." Core social programs developed later in America than in Europe and in a few notable cases, such as national health insurance, they did not materialize at all (Howard 1993: 403). Americans, however, have a somewhat different view. Not only are they generally less positive than Europeans about welfare as a whole (see below for an "American view" of Europe), but they display surprisingly similar—that is, less than enthusiastic—sentiments even on matters that command very high levels of American support, such as retirement benefits, health care, jobs, and housing (Shapiro and Young 1989: 69). Quite simply, Americans start from a different position.

So much is clear. A number of additional factors must, however, be taken into account if the American case is to be fully understood. These include the "hidden side" of welfare—that is, the indirect rather than direct tools of social policy, such as loans, loan guarantees, and tax expenditures, all of which abound in the United States (Howard 1993: 403). Equally important is an awareness that the welfare sector in American society is growing rather than shrinking, if one includes in this notion programs that incorporate market principles into welfare provision.[15] Thirdly, on matters of educational opportunity, assistance, and spending, American policies are in some ways stronger and more developed than their European counterparts—a manifestation, once again, of American individualism, in the sense that the focus is more on the equality of opportunity than the equality of outcomes (Shapiro and Young 1989: 69).

How though does this relate to the question of religion? It is at this point that the "faith-based initiatives" of George W. Bush become important—that is, a set of initiatives introduced in the President's first term, which included a program of government funding for churches and other houses of worship, by means of which social services would be offered to Americans in need.[16] The program has been highly controversial. For a start, it constitutes a bold challenge to the principle of church–state separation, in the sense that it removes the restrictions which normally apply to funding attached to any religious institution (e.g. that an individual should attend a worship service in order to receive aid from a particular organization) (Davis 2003a). But quite apart from questions of constitutionality, the notion of faith-based initiatives has provoked a wide-ranging debate about welfare provision in American society and the place of the churches in this.

On the one hand, it is possible to see these programs as a natural extension of what the hundreds and thousands of American congregations do everyday. Much of what is normally considered welfare is already taking place amongst groups of people who come together for primarily religious reasons. The move towards better-funded and officially recognized welfare provision on the part of religious groups is, therefore, a step in the right direction; it builds creatively on work already in hand, and maximizes the potential of networks already in place. Why reinvent the wheel? Others, however, are much more wary, recognizing that faith-based initiatives raise difficult moral as well as constitutional questions. For example: to what extent should government policies reflect religious values? More precisely, to what extent should faith-based organizations be able to influence those to whom they are extending help? What, moreover, is the connection between such organizations and the interests of the Bush administration itself, not least its specifically religious motivations? And—always assuming that satisfactory answers can be found to the above—how should faith-based initiatives be put into practice? Should government-funded faith-based organizations be allowed to employ only individuals who share their religious beliefs? More importantly, would such a policy endorse, consciously or not, a notion of funding that supports religious discrimination? The fact, finally, that the president introduced the initiative through a series of Executive Orders has sparked a continuing and at times acrimonious debate about the democratic nature of the entire procedure (Roberts-DeGennaro 2006). This last is a particularly thorny issue.

It is hardly surprising that counter-movements have begun to appear. One such—the emotively named "Theocracy Watch" (a public information project of the Center for Religion, Ethics and Social Policy at Cornell University)—is clearly very concerned, seeing faith-based initiatives as one aspect of a much more dangerous phenomenon: the undermining of democracy by a religiously motivated Republican Party, which is something to be avoided at all costs. Most interesting from the point of view of this chapter is a revealing quotation on the website of this organization, which is taken from a speech made by George W. Bush in 2004. This reads: "We want to fund programs that save Americans one soul at a time."[17] The reference to American individualism could hardly be plainer. Less political, and rather more informative, is the careful work of Ram Cnaan and his colleagues at the University of Pennsylvania, whose publications (Cnaan 2002; Cnaan et al. 2006; Boddie and Cnaan 2007) fill an important gap in the literature, supplying much needed empirical information about how faith-based initiatives work in practice and how we might evaluate their success or failure. Do they, for instance, have the necessary tools to become significant providers in the social service arena? And, assuming that they do, how might the professionalization of such services affect the spirit of volunteerism so evident in America's religious institutions? It is too early to draw any definite conclusions.

The relationship between religion and welfare in Europe is very different. Just how different can be discovered in an article which brings together a number of themes not only from this chapter but from those which precede it (Muller 1997). Its author (a president emeritus of Johns Hopkins University) demonstrates not only a quintessentially American view of the welfare state in Europe, but the radical divergence in thinking between Europeans and at least some Americans regarding the desirability, or otherwise, of a politico-religious lobby. The two moreover are related. According to Muller, religion survives in the United States as a serious force in politics, notably in the form of a conservative religious movement—explicitly committed to traditional Christian values and vigorously opposed to social and political liberalism. Here, in fact, is the New Christian Right just described, resistant amongst other things to the promotion of social justice through "big government." It follows that the absence of a similar movement in Europe will impoverish the political life of the continent. Without such a force, Muller argues, a liberal orthodoxy is institutionalized far deeper in the structures of the welfare state—and even inside the churches—in Europe than it is in the United States. In a nutshell, the non-existence of a powerful religious lobby and the existence of a welfare state are two sides of the same "European" coin. Both, moreover, impede initiative.

The majority of Europeans, of course, have a very different view (as do many Americans); they are profoundly supportive not only of a moderately comprehensive welfare system, but of the political values that this represents. The relative absence of a religious right becomes, therefore, an advantage, not a disadvantage, revealing a very different set of assumptions. In the United States, conservative religion is seen by many as a positive factor which counteracts the liberal thinking of European welfare enthusiasts. In Europe, it is the welfare state that is constructed positively, to the point perhaps of replacing the need for religion. Care, both for individuals and for communities, is delivered by the state. There is no room in this conceptualization for the complex networks of support associated with America's multiple, flexible, and market-driven religious organizations.

Is this an accurate view of Europe? The question will be addressed with reference to an ongoing comparative project on religion and welfare in eight European societies (Welfare and Religion in a European Perspective, commonly known as WREP).[18] The story begins with the gradual development of the welfare system as a distinct area of activity in the different countries of Europe, an institutional shift which is inseparable from the process of secularization. Indeed the separating out of welfare mirrors almost exactly the establishment of the public school system described in the previous section—the more so in the sense that the process takes place differently in different European societies, leading to distinctive welfare regimes alongside distinctive educational provision. Regarding the former, specialists in social policy will immediately categorize these differences into different welfare clusters—the work of Gøsta Esping-Anderson (1989) offers an excellent example. For the sociologist of religion, however, an additional point is immediately clear: the patterns that emerge relate very closely to the differences observed by Martin in his work on secularization. In this sense, therefore, this chapter becomes—once again—a continuation of the story begun in Chapter 3.

The WREP project furnishes rich data in this field, which can be used in different ways. First to exemplify the different models of welfare in different parts of Europe: the social democracies of the Nordic countries, the rather particular French case, the influence of Catholic social teaching on developments in southern Europe, a distinctive Orthodox example, and last but not least the British case—pulled as ever in two directions. In each situation, a particular variant of the welfare state emerges, as a similar goal (the separating out of welfare from the influence of the churches and the creation of an autonomous sphere with its own institutional norms) is achieved, or semi-achieved, in somewhat different ways. Interestingly the role of both theology and ecclesiology in determining these pathways is increasingly recognized in the literature (Van Kersbergen and Manow forthcoming). Even more important, however, are the underlying sentiments: European populations are of one mind in thinking that the state should take responsibility in this area. That finding emerges from all the case studies in the WREP project. The fact that the churches are still doing much of the work is seen as a necessary feature of European life, but not "how it should be." The project's respondents are, nonetheless, realistic: given that the situation is less than perfect, it is just as well that the churches are there, if only to fill the gaps. It follows that their contributions tend to be welcomed rather than rejected even in societies where the welfare state is more rather than less developed.

So far, so good. Towards the end of the twentieth century, however, a number of factors have come together to question many of these assumptions. Some of these factors come from outside. European societies are as subject to the swings in the global economy as anyone else and, from the 1970s on, almost all European nations experienced both a downturn in economic growth, and a corresponding rise in unemployment. Coincidentally, demographic profiles are altering, leading (as in all advanced economies) to an increase both in the numbers and in the proportion of elderly people. Taken together, these trends are beginning to undermine the foundations on which the provision of welfare is constructed: not only with respect to the adequacy of the services themselves but, more radically, how these services are financed. The problem is easily stated: will the proportion of people active in the economy remain sufficient to support those who, for whatever reason, are not able to work? Add to this the marked prolongation of education that is part and parcel of a post-industrial economy and the implications are clear. No longer is it possible for most European societies to meet the obligations of welfare as these were understood in the immediate post-war period.

A noticeable change in political philosophy—a rowing back from the notion that the state is responsible for the provision of welfare from the cradle to the grave—is one reaction to these shifts. As ever, European societies have set about this in different ways, the most striking of which occurred in Britain in the 1980s. The Thatcher government not only instigated radical reforms, it evolved an ideology to legitimate such changes. The debate, however, is not only ideological. If the state is no longer able, or even willing, to provide a comprehensive system of welfare for its citizens, who is to be responsible for this task? It is clear that the churches, amongst others, have a role to play in these changes. Initial observations from the WREP project reveal, moreover, an interesting theme: that the factors which were present when the initial differentiation of responsibilities took place are still in place as the new situation begins to emerge. Or to put the same point in a different way, the process of de-differentiation is as nationally specific as its predecessor. Hence the possibility of a relatively easy resumption of the welfare role on the part of the churches in some parts of Europe, and a much more difficult one in others. Three examples will suffice. In Italy or Greece, a very incomplete separation of powers in the first place has meant that the line between state and church remains essentially fluid. It can move back and forth as the situation demands. In France, in contrast, the secular state remains firmly in control, so much so that the researcher engaged on the French case had difficulty persuading the public authorities to cooperate at all in a project that paid attention to religion. In Finland finally, the very particular conditions of the recession in the early 1990s, as the Russian market collapsed, have led not only to a noticeable rise in the welfare roles undertaken by the churches but to a rise in their popularity as a result.

Considerably more could be said with respect both to this project and to its successor (Welfare and Values in Europe, or WaVE) which will extend the work in two ways: first to the minority religions of Europe, paying particular attention to the Muslim population, and second to the selected countries in the formerly communist parts of Europe where the positions of state and church are necessarily different. The latter lie, for the most part, beyond the remit of this discussion, though their attitudes to the market are interesting. The former—inevitably linked to the question of immigration—will form a central theme of our fourth and final variation.

Before turning to this, one further, and by now familiar, point is important. In beginning to appreciate the limitations of the welfare state, is Europe—or more accurately, parts of Europe—becoming more like the United States? In other words, are forms of faith-based initiatives making their presence felt in Europe as well as the United States? The question must at least be asked. Answers will vary, but one might be found in the following. This is not Americanization, but a distinctively European mutation—nicely captured, in welfare as in religion, as a shift from obligation to consumption. State provision is not quite as secure as it used to be; as a result, a mixed economy, if not exactly a free market, is beginning to emerge. The two fields moreover are becoming less and less distinct. The churches (both old and new) are growing in importance as welfare providers; at the same time welfare is less averse to the religious or the spiritual than it used to be. The situation merits careful, continuing and, above all, inter-disciplinary attention.

Notes

1 The place of political parties and the family will be considered in the following chapter.

2 The text of the First Amendment reads as follows: "Congress shall make no law respecting an establishment of religion, or prohibiting the free exercise thereof; or abridging the freedom of speech, or of the press; or the right of the people peaceably to assemble, and to petition the Government for a redress of grievances."

3 In 2002, in *Zelmans v. Simmons-Harris*, the Supreme Court addressed the constitutionality of school vouchers and ruled to allow the use of vouchers for redemption at religious schools: local governments could provide such funds, although they would not be required to do so.

4   Thirty-six other states have similar bans on the use of public funds. See: www.firstamendmentcenter.org /news.aspx?id=12755 (accessed 6 May 2008)

5   This can be found in the ruling of *Engel v. Vitale* (1962), which struck down a non-denominational prayer written by the New York Board of Regents for official use in the public schools of New York.

6   A longer discussion in French can be found in Hervieu-Léger (2001a).

7   That is, the chair in the "Histoire et Sociologie de la Laïcité," at the Ecole Pratique des Hautes Etudes, at the Sorbonne. Jean Baubérot is a prolific writer in this field—see for example Baubérot 1990; 1997; 2005.

8   In fact, the pledge issue raises two potential problems of constitutionality: first, can students be compelled to recite the pledge without infringing on their First Amendment rights; and second, is the inclusion of "under God" in the text a violation of the establishment clause? The first problem was addressed by the Supreme Court in 1940 (*Minersville School District v. Gobitis*), when the court ruled that students in public schools could be compelled to recite the pledge, and then in 1943 (*West Virginia State Board of Education v. Barnette*), when the court deemed the compulsory recitation a violation of the First Amendment. The second problem is raised in the 2004 *Elk Grove Unified School District v. Newdow* case in California, and has already been addressed.

9   The "Lemon test" was developed by the United States Supreme Court in the *Lemon v. Kurtzman* (1971) case regarding the reimbursement (with public funds) for teachers' salaries, textbooks, and instruction materials in non-public (in practice, mainly Catholic) schools. According to the Lemon test, actions are deemed as in violation of the establishment clause if (a) they do not carry a secular purpose, (b) they have an obvious effect of either advancing or inhibiting religion, and (c) they result in an "excessive entanglement" with religion.

10 Harriet Miers, George W. Bush's second nominee to the Supreme Court, eventually withdrew her candidature in face of serious resistance to her stance on abortion. Ms. Miers's views on abortion were insufficiently secure to gain the support of the conservative lobby within the Republican Party.

11 There are other fundamental differences between the nature of the ECtHR and the United States Supreme Court which limit their comparability: one of these is the fact that the rulings of the ECtHR are binding only to signatories of the European Convention of Human Rights. Quite apart from this, the ECtHR does not correspond to a strict and fixed geographical gambit—it continually changes, reflecting the expansion of the European integration project. In the present discussion, the focus will be restricted to the European Union and its member states as signatories of the European Convention on Human Rights and, accordingly, as subject to the rulings of the ECtHR.

12 This is not the view, of course, of the more cosmopolitan "Swedes" (see Chapter 2)—vide the constitutional battles already described.

13 In England and Wales, the argument turns on the need for fairness. If the Catholics and the Anglicans are permitted "voluntary-aided" schools, can the

same privilege be denied to other faith communities whose schools meet the necessary educational criteria (see Jackson 2004; 2007)?

14 Not everyone, however, was happy with this arrangement. See the judgement of the ECtHR in favour of the Norwegian Humanist Association and against the Norwegian state (*Folgero and others v. Norway*, n° 15472/02, 29 June 2007). The case turned on the right of exemption from classes in religious education.

15 For a discussion of this point see Bordas (2001).

16 The White House Office of Faith-Based and Community Initiatives (OFBCI) was established by Executive Order of George W. Bush in January 2001. Details of the program can be found on the White House website, at: http://www.whitehouse.gov/government/fbci/president-initiative.html (accessed 6 May 2008).

17 See: http://www.theocracywatch.org/faith_base.htm (accessed 6 May 2008).

18 WREP is a research project coordinated by the Uppsala Centre for the Study of Religion and Society and is funded by the Bank of Sweden Tercentenary Foundation. The research covers the cases of Sweden, Norway, Finland, England, Germany, France, Italy, and Greece. WaVE is a European Commission FP6-funded project which builds on the WREP study as indicated (shifting the focus from majority to minority religions, and including the cases of Latvia, Poland, Croatia, and Romania).

Chapter 6

Variation Four:
Religion and Social Difference

Our final variation takes as its starting point Max Weber's story of the dentist, introduced in Chapter 2 (pp. 20–21). The essential point is the following: why was the European dentist so bewildered by his American patient's reference to religion as a proxy for financial security? Keeping this in mind, the chapter is structured as follows. It looks first at the ways in which religion relates to the core indices of social difference: social class, ethnicity, gender, and age. Interestingly the first two display very marked differences between Europe and the United States; the latter, however, are much more similar. A second theme runs parallel, and continues the discussion of the previous variation. It introduces two further institutions that have to do with the maintenance or otherwise of religious vitality. These are the political configurations that can be found in Europe but not in America (more precisely the role of socialism and socialist parties in the history of Europe) and the significance of the family in the handing on of religious identities. The former arises out the discussion of social class; the latter draws together a whole cluster of variables relating to gender, generation, and the different demographics of newly arrived populations.

Before starting, however, a crucial observation must be noted, drawing yet again on David Martin's *General Theory of Secularization* (1978). Religion cuts vertically into American society as each group of new arrivals brings with it its own religious package; in Europe, the patterns are horizontal—a direct consequence of the collusions of religion and power over many centuries. A short walk round any American city will confirm the former. At the same time it will reveal the huge diversity both within and between the myriad denominations which constitute religious life in America. Irish, Italian, and Polish Catholics, to name but the most obvious, each have their own centers of worship and community—now joined by increasing numbers of Latino congregations. Protestants, given their fissiparous nature, are even more diverse and are present on every block—some very visible, some less so.[1] An essentially similar pattern, moreover, can be found in the different "interest groups" of American religion as families, singles, professionals, seniors, activists, and so on create and sustain forms of religion that are suited to their particular life styles. In both respects, religion sinks deeply into the fabric of American society.

In Europe, the embedding of religion into society is quite different. Its primarily horizontal nature derives very directly from the "official" status of Christianity as a state religion, first in Europe as a whole, and then in its constituent nations. Here one church dominated the territory (both national and local), integrally linked historically to the power structures that surrounded it—indeed in some places it still is. The system as such gradually disintegrated, though more so in some parts of Europe than in others. The result, however, is complex—a point well-illustrated in the subtle combinations of vicarious religion and religious choice described in previous chapters. With this in mind, it is important to pay attention to the default positions which have emerged in either case. In Europe residual membership of the historic tradition remains the norm; in the United States, active voluntary membership of a free-standing religious group is the dominant model. Both are connected to social class, but in different ways.

Religion and Social Class

The discussion starts from the following question: what, in a particular context, are the markers of social difference and how do these relate to religion? Hence the significance of the dentist story: most Americans would grasp the reference to religion as an indicator of economic success (and therefore reliability); not so a European. How can this be explained?

The first point is clear: social class differences exist in both European and American society but they are differently configured. They have, moreover, a distinctive impact: American society is plainly more mobile than its European equivalent, but not perfectly so. And in both cases, class is criss-crossed by a variety of other variables (including ethnicity, gender and age). What, then, is the role of religion and—more precisely—of religious vitality in these different configurations? Taking the European case first, there is a demonstrable pattern in the churchgoing constituency: regular churchgoing is a middle-class activity across much of the continent, though more so in the north than the south.[2] Indeed there have been moments when respectability rather than conviction has been the primary motivation for church attendance. Here was one place where you could both see and be seen. Nominal indices of religiousness, however, are different, and penetrate much further down the social scale, leading to a "classic" European pattern: until moderately recently many working-class people assumed membership of the historic churches, but did not attend them. Belief existed, but was seldom articulated. Indeed too much activity in either respect was considered hypocritical and was expressed in the following, oft-repeated phrases: "You don't need to be a Christian to go to church" or "I am just as good a Christian as she (the churchgoer) is" (Ahern and Davie 1987; Davie 1994).

That, of course, is not the whole story: women are consistently more religious than men on whatever measure is used (see below). Conversely—and to elaborate the point already made in Chapter 4—all such indices are particularly low amongst two very different groups of men: on the one hand intellectuals, and on the other the manual working-class. Having said this, the non-practice of the working class is—and in some ways always has been—counter-balanced by new arrivals. In nineteenth-century Britain, for example, Irish immigration invigorated the Catholic Church leading not only to distinctive politico-religious alignments, but to levels of practice long since lost in the dominant church. A century or so later, the story is repeating itself, as Afro-Caribbeans arrive in the major cities of the United Kingdom—an opportunity squandered by the established church to the advantage of more independent communities.[3] Quite clearly, the twenty-first century will be different again as yet further mutations occur. Stubbornly resistant, however, are the deep-seated links between religion and power which have endured for more than a millennium. Their influence is permanent—so too the mentalities that go with them. The connections with vicarious religion have already been established (pp. 26, 39–40).

Neither the links nor the mentalities exist in the American case, where in constitutional terms political and religious power are rigorously separate. With respect to social class, two rather different things follow from this. The first concerns the complex relationships between (a) churchgoing in general—where social class differences are much less evident, and (b) the ways in which specific denominations become *de facto* badges of social class. Each point requires expansion. The first derives from the different embedding of religion in American society already discussed. Each community brought with it to the United States its own form of religion which became an important means of support as the group in question found its feet in a new society. The habit continued; indeed in some ways it reversed the European model from which it sprang—in the sense that Europeans, of all classes, became more rather than less practicing as they set down their roots in the United States (Casanova 2007). Churchgoing, it follows, is not a middle-class activity in the United States; indeed there is evidence to the contrary in so far as it is inversely rather than directly related to levels of income (Norris and Inglehart 2004: 108–10).

The situation, however, continues to evolve, at which point a second feature of the American landscape becomes important. That is the phenomenon known as "switching" in which Americans chop and change their denominational allegiance for a wide variety of reasons, both religious and less so. Among the latter, undoubtedly, are reasons of social difference: moving up (or down) the social scale may well involve a change in denomination—hence the second anecdote in Berger's introductory chapter in which an aspiring colleague reveals a corresponding shift in religious allegiance (pp. 20–21). The same story displays, moreover, the infinitely subtle rules of the game—not least the size of the steps that can be made at any one time. It is not wise to be too ambitious.

So much for religion and social class as such. The second consequence of the separation of church and state in the United States is somewhat different and concerns politics as much as class—a discussion in which the role of political parties as carriers of secular identity moves center stage. Once again it must start with the European case—more precisely with the reactions to the collusions of religion and power in Europe that have already been described. As Europeans rejected authoritarian regimes, they rejected the religious legitimations that went with these and vice versa. As ever, the quintessential case is the French; elsewhere the reactions are more nuanced. Indeed at this point the discussion mirrors very closely the section devoted to the Enlightenment. What emerged, however, in much of Catholic Europe was a religio-political divide with a conservative set of forces on one side (including the churches) and a more radical constituency on the other, within which anti-clericalism became a distinctive component. Or to put the same point more forcibly, the political Left in Europe in both its extreme (communist) and less extreme (socialist) forms includes more than a touch of secularism.

This is not the place to explore in detail either the policies or the practices of the communist parties of the former Soviet Union and its subordinate states towards religion. Suffice it to say that the anti-religious ideologies of all these translated into actions that can be placed along a continuum from harassment at one end to outright persecution at the other—all of which have become discredited since the collapse of the Berlin Wall. Rather more central to the argument of this section are the political philosophies of the socialist parties of western Europe, which—though anti-clerical in sentiment—stopped short at outright intimidation. Such parties have become important carriers of secularist thinking, especially when their principal opposition was some form of Catholic party. The result is a complex amalgam of religion and politics across much of Europe as the politics of class become inextricably linked with religion (mostly Catholicism) on the one hand and secularism on the other. In terms of the comparison with the United States, the difference is striking: neither communism, nor socialism exist in the United States as an effective political force, one reason being, surely, the entirely different configurations of church and state that existed from the outset.

That does not mean that politics and religion do not mix in the United States: they most certainly do—a point developed at length in previous chapters. But the ways in which this happens are quite different, leading, as ever, to mutual incomprehension on each side of the Atlantic. Europeans remain bemused by the presence of religion in its American forms and by its influence on moral issues in particular. Americans, conversely, are bewildered by the presence in Europe of explicitly secular socio-political ideologies. Paradoxically, or perhaps not, the former exist where church and state were deemed separate; the latter where they were not.

Once again—in what has become a recurring refrain—the British case is different. More precisely the Labour Party in the United Kingdom is distinct from its continental equivalents. The point is contentious, but the old adage, that the British Labour Party owes more to Methodism than to Marx, has truth in it—whether or not you think that this is a good thing or a bad one (Johnson 2000). Indeed the whole politico-religious package is turned on its head in the sense that not only Methodists, but Catholics (a constituency dominated by Irish immigrants) supported the political Left in Britain rather than the Right. The situation is complicated further by the presence of minority parties, frequently associated with various expressions of non conformity, in the smaller nations of the United Kingdom—that is, in Scotland, Wales, and Northern Ireland. The last of these has proved particularly intractable, but it is not a story in which anti-clericalism, in its classic forms, plays any part. Northern Ireland, as ever, deserves a book in it own right. Returning instead to the European mainstream, it is important to pursue the question of minorities in more detail. Their impact on both politics and religion is considerable.

Immigration and Ethnicity

Many of the elements in this discussion have already appeared in previous chapters, bearing in mind that there are two sides to the question. The first concerns the impact of minority religions on the political scene in Europe; the second relates to the unpreparedness of European intellectuals to deal with this. This section puts both of these points in context.

The bare bones of the story are clear enough. As the dominant economies of western Europe, that is Britain, France, West Germany, and the Netherlands, took off after World War II, there was an urgent need for new sources of labor. Unsurprisingly, each of the societies in question looked in a different direction in order to meet this need, and wherever possible to their former colonies. Hence in Britain, there were two quite distinct influxes—one from the West Indies and one from the Indian sub-continent. A similar process took place across the Channel, bringing into metropolitan France a more homogeneous population from North Africa. West Germany, with no ex-colonies, looked in a different direction—this time to Turkey and the former Yugoslavia. The Netherlands, finally, encouraged immigration from former colonial territories, but also from Turkey and Morocco. What emerged was a sizeable, economically motivated, immigrant population across much of Europe, within which a diverse Muslim presence has become an increasingly important factor. This constituency is now in its third generation; in each generation, moreover, different issues are raised—specific combinations of assimilation and difference.

In the last decade of the twentieth century something rather different has taken place. European countries that until very recently had been places of emigration—notably Spain, Italy, and Greece—now became countries of immigration; so too the Nordic societies. The reasons are many and include expanding economies, falling birth rates, and—particularly in the north of Europe—the comprehensive welfare state mentioned in Chapter 5 (clearly a pull factor for some). The demographic aspects of this discussion are crucial; they are also complex. What will happen, for example, when those who work today (the newly arrived), in order that Europeans may enjoy generous welfare provision (most importantly their pensions), become themselves dependent in one way or another on the system that they now sustain? It is at this point that the tensions begin to show, just as they did in Britain, France, West Germany, and the Netherlands, as the 1960s merged into the rather less prosperous decade that followed. Two things happened at once at this point. On the one hand, groups of people who were initially viewed as migrant workers—people who came and went as the economy required—were becoming, along with their families, a permanent feature of European societies. At precisely the same moment the economic indicators turned downwards, unemployment rose and the competition for jobs, houses, and school places became increasingly acute. Unsurprisingly those Europeans whose economic positions were most vulnerable resented the newly arrived populations, leading in the 1970s and 1980s to extensive urban unrest in which racial and ethnic tensions played a significant role.

The phrase "racial and ethnic" is important. These difficulties were not considered as in any way related to religion—a construction which fitted easily into the worldviews of European academics and the policy-makers that worked with them. Both, quite correctly, could follow their liberal consciences and support the victims of ethnic discrimination. Bit by bit, however, the situation altered as the newly arrived in Europe began to assert their presence in unexpected ways—demanding, amongst other things, that Europeans take their religious, as well as their ethnic, identities seriously. This was not so easy. Indeed, it is at this point that we rejoin the narrative in Chapter 4 and the difficulties envisaged in that discussion. On the one hand can be found a whole series of episodes that reveal the growing importance of religion, and on the other are the intellectuals disconcerted by what is happening. The former are unlikely to diminish; the latter are hovering uneasily between denial and consternation. Neither reaction is helpful.

There is insufficient space in this chapter to describe in detail the various episodes that have brought these issues to a head—they will be referred to only in so far as they illustrate particular points in the argument. They include, however, the debates surrounding the episodes already listed on p. 54: the preamble to the European Constitution, the Rushdie controversy in Britain, the *affaire du foulard* in France, the murders of Pim Fortuyn and Theo van Gogh in the Netherlands (together with the subsequent defection of Hirsi Ali to the United States), the future over the Danish cartoons of Mohammed, and the bombings in the transport systems of both Madrid and London in 2004 and 2005 respectively. More detailed accounts can be found in Davie (2007b and 2007c) and in the burgeoning literature in the field, in itself an index of growing concern.[4] Central to this discussion will be, first, the themes that are common to all these controversies, and second, the contrasts with the United States. Both are described with the utmost clarity in Casanova's contribution to a collection which should become required reading by academics and policy-makers alike (Casanova 2007).[5] The following paragraphs draw very directly on this work.

Casanova's analysis sits squarely within the approach set out in this book, in that it recognizes right from the start the contrasts between Europe and the United States in terms of both institutional structures and philosophical approaches. The notion of European secularity is central to his argument, including an insistence that this is, in many respects, a self-fulfilling prophecy. What though are the consequences for European approaches to minority religions? There is more than one answer to this question given that each country in Europe has addressed the issue in different ways, drawing as ever on the particular features of the host society. More than anything else, however, Casanova—like Habermas—demonstrates a lack of reciprocity in the argument, a point already noted (pp. 61–3). Conservative religious people are expected to be tolerant of forms of behavior that many of them (including Muslims) find difficult: explicit forms of sexuality, same-sex unions, and blasphemy offer the most obvious examples. The reverse, however, is not the case. Secular liberals simply refuse, it seems, to tolerate religious behavior or cultural customs that run counter to their cherished ideals. The Rushdie controversy provides a revealing illustration.

Indeed the most crucial point in the whole affair came two years or so after it initially broke, at the moment when Rushdie claimed to have "embraced" Islam. With every appearance of sincerity, he declared himself a Muslim (*The Guardian*, 17 January 1991), apologizing to his co-religionists for the problems caused by *The Satanic Verses* and acknowledging that some passages were offensive to believers. Financial contributions from his royalties would be made to those who had suffered injury as a result of protests—in other words reparations would be made. The attempt to build bridges seemed genuine enough and brought some comfort to the Muslim community. The gesture, however, provoked a torrent of abuse from the opposing camp; the outrage of the secular liberals could hardly be contained, revealing an alarming illogicality at the heart of their campaign. Muslims should be tolerant of offensive books, but liberals cannot tolerate the writer who expresses an affinity with Islam. Tolerance was clearly a social construct, to be applied in some cases but not in others.

Something rather similar has happened in the Netherlands. In this case, there is evident tension between a dominant, liberal lifestyle and the distinctly illiberal policies that have been put in place to protect this. The Dutch, more precisely, are known for their advanced positions on a whole range of issues, including homosexuality, euthanasia, and the use of soft drugs. It follows that only those ready to accept such policies can be admitted to their ranks. The "others," who hold more traditional views, are much less welcome, to the point—if necessary—of exclusion. The irony lies in the following: to what extent is it possible to protect the values associated with liberalism by being illiberal? Taken too far, surely, such policies are likely to undermine the very cause that they seek to promote. So far, however, the irony is lost on a constituency who—consciously or not—construct their discourse differently. Not only are they defending the majority view, they are defending what is "right." Casanova puts this as follows:

> What makes the intolerant tyranny of the secular, liberal majority justifiable in principle is not just the democratic principle of majority rule, but rather the secularist teleological assumption built into theories of modernization that one set of norms is reactionary, fundamentalist, and antimodern, while the other set is progressive, liberal, and modern. (Casanova 2007: 65)

It is for this reason that the presence of some, if not all, religious minorities becomes so problematic for many Europeans. Simply by being there, they

bring to the attention of Europeans a series of unresolved issues which—
for decades, if not centuries—have been placed in the realm of the private.
To the consternation of many, these are back in the public sphere.

So far the discussion has concentrated largely on the tensions between
secularism and Islam. How, in this situation, do the Christian churches
react? The answers, as ever, are varied and depend to some extent on
degrees of commitment. Active or practicing Christians, for example,
are more likely to assert the primacy of their own faith as a cornerstone
of European civilization. That is understandable. In terms of motivation,
however, there are noticeable differences in this constituency. On the one
hand can be found a marked hostility to Muslims, provoked very often
by fear, and expressed in negative, sometimes very destructive, terms.
On the other—and more intriguingly—there is, at least in some quarters,
a transparent admiration for Islam. Here, in effect, are those inspired by
Muslim success in placing religion back on the public agenda, seeing
in this shift new opportunities for all peoples of faith. Christians should
follow suit. Whatever their respective motivations, both groups are
likely to find themselves working alongside the Muslim constituency in
opposition to those who assert secularism as a primary value of Europe.
It was precisely this combination that became increasingly explicit in the
debate concerning the preamble to the European Constitution in 2003; it
is likely to recur in any event that recalls the founding principles of the
European Union.

If a minority of Christians see in Islam either a threat or a role model
for religious activities, the majority are less convinced. Disconcerted by
the seriously religious of all kinds, most Europeans (Christian, Muslim,
and secular) are happy to live and let live. "A plague on both your houses"
becomes an entirely understandable reaction, reminiscent of the response
to generations of religious strife. Never again must Europeans come to
blows about religion, and never again must religion become a barrier to
progress. Such reactions, however, fail in important ways to appreciate
the significance of the issues that are arising in Europe with alarming
regularity. These require a more pro-active approach. The more so in that
many of these episodes have a global resonance. It is simply not possible
for European societies, and the Muslim communities within them, to live
in isolation from the disturbing events that are taking place in other parts of
the world. The Rushdie controversy, for example, became infinitely more
difficult to resolve, following the *fatwa* pronounced on a British citizen by
an Iranian ayatollah.

The underlying question becomes, therefore, the following: who will
give way to whom in these very difficult issues? On the one hand, there
are those who take the "when in Rome, do as the Romans do" approach.

Muslims, or indeed members of any other minority, who want to live in the West must behave as Westerners. This is fine in theory, but pushed too far, it effectively means that such people can no longer practice their faith in any meaningful way. At the other extreme, a few (very few) religious enthusiasts want, it seems, to hold Western society to ransom in demanding special privileges for themselves and the communities that they represent. Here there is a whole spectrum of possibilities, including, it must be said, acts of terrorism. Most people, of course, lie somewhere between the two, though exactly where will vary from place to place to place, group to group, and person to person. Finding a way through these dilemmas in terms of policy-making has become an urgent and very demanding political task. It is more likely to be successful, however, if careful attention is given to the concepts underpinning the debate and if the communities most closely involved are heard with respect and on their own terms (the discussion must be about religion, not about "something else"—race or ethnicity for example). In short, issues involving religious identities become more, not less, difficult to solve, if religion as such is proscribed as a category in public life.

That is unlikely to be the case in the United States where the whole debate is very different, to the point where religion, an essentially positive feature, becomes an important means through which the much more destructive dynamic of racism, or racialization, can be neutralized (Casanova 2007). It is for this reason that those recently arrived in America will not only claim, but exploit a religious identity, seeing this as the means to gain a foothold in their chosen society. Here, in other words, is yet another reason for the process that we have already observed: immigrants are likely to increase rather than decrease their religious activity once they arrive in the United States. In so doing, they conform to the churchgoing norm. Conversely, they are not expected to keep either their language or their nationality—an anomaly noted by Herberg in his classic division of American society into Protestant, Catholic, and Jew (Herberg 1965).

Conforming to the norm means, however, conforming to the denominational model. Without the organizational and, above all, legal trappings of a denomination, it is almost impossible to operate as a religious group in American society. That all-pervasive model, however, is easier for some religious groups than others. Clearly, it is relatively straightforward for the myriad Christian denominations that continue to arrive almost by the day; it is rather more difficult for those whose traditions are different. That, in turn, raises a second issue: while Muslims constitute the great majority of new arrivals in Europe, this is not true in the United States. In the latter, Christians (of different kinds and from very different global regions) make up more than 70 per cent of new arrivals; the Muslim proportion is less than 10 per cent

(Casanova 2007: 79). It provokes none the less some interesting questions. One such is the link between American attitudes to Catholicism in the nineteenth century and attitudes to Islam some hundred years later. Both have been viewed as profoundly un-American, in the sense that both are, or are felt to be, resistant to the republican ideal. The changing fortunes of Catholicism in America have been well documented. Will the same, essentially positive, story be true of Islam? It is not impossible, but the impact of 9/11 has taken its toll; so too the war in Iraq.

The debate, no doubt, will continue, one sign of which is the rash of books in the field—herein, at least, there is a similarity to Europe.[6] Equally important are the responses of a number of academic institutions, who have established centers for study and dialogue.[7] Not everyone, however, welcomes such conciliatory approaches. Indeed as Casanova himself remarks, two very different tendencies emerge. On the one hand, there is a real effort to be inclusive, an attitude symbolized in some circles by a shift in vocabulary from Judeo-Christian to Abrahamic. Rather more difficult, however, are the reactions of some, though by no means all, Evangelicals—among whom can be found an alarming tendency to see in the growing visibility of Islam the principal threat both to the United States as such, and more broadly to Christian civilization. It is in these quarters, moreover, that the transformation of cold-war anti-communist rhetoric into reinvigorated anti-Islamic sentiments is most noticeable. It is encouraged, of course, by those who see in the State of Israel fulfilment of the biblical narrative.

More could be said on all these issues. As a conclusion to this section, however, it is interesting to note the views of the more extreme Evangelical constituency in the United States towards what is happening in Europe. This, moreover, is a discourse in which the connections between Evangelicals on the one hand, and conservative Catholics on the other, becomes abundantly clear; indeed it provides a crucial thread in the analysis. The argument is constructed as follows. Two things are happening at once in Europe: first there is marked decline in birth rates right across the continent, a fact which is not disputed. European women are choosing not only to delay childbearing; increasingly, they are choosing not to have children at all. And even those who do raise families are having fewer pregnancies overall, to the point that, in almost every country in Europe, the birth rate has fallen below replacement levels. At the same time, the Muslim population is growing, not only in terms of immigration, but also in terms of family size, which—among first generation immigrants at least— is markedly higher than in the host population. Putting these two "trends" together, there is plenty of space for extrapolation, not to say panic, in a discourse in which the notion of "Eurabia" is increasingly present. From this perspective, Europe is losing its identity and will become, surely if not quite immediately, an extension of the Muslim (Arab) world, thus completing a project that was initiated many centuries ago—thwarted by European resistance, first at Poitiers (in the eighth century) and then at Vienna (some nine hundred years later).

There is a burgeoning literature in this field—notably the work of Lewis (1997; 2003), Bawer (2006), and Weigel (2006). The last of these, interestingly, is also the biographer of John-Paul II, a towering figure in the recent history of Europe. Known first and foremost for his resistance to communism, John-Paul was equally a staunch supporter of traditional family codes, including the childrearing role of women. Such policies continue under Benedict XVI, who remains attentive not only to the traditional patterns of family life, but also to the central importance of Christianity in Europe—past, present, and future. The two, moreover, are related. Hence the very real dismay, whenever the status of Christianity is undermined in public discussions in Europe; this especially if there is a hint that this place might be taken by someone else.

Very different people have been drawn together in these exchanges: conservative Catholics on both sides of the Atlantic (worried both about birth rates and about European identity), Evangelical Protestants in the United States (who need a focus for their views now the cold war is over), and—finally—secular philosophers who resist relativism of all kinds. This last is represented in the recent collaboration between the then Cardinal Ratzinger and Marcello Pera—the former President of the Italian Senate, a member of Forza Italia, a philosopher of science, and a self-confessed unbeliever. Their conversations (two lectures and two letters) were subsequently published in a volume, the title of which is revealing: *Without Roots: Europe, Relativism, Christianity, Islam* (Ratzinger and Pera 2006). Without roots, by which they mean Christian roots, Europe is vulnerable and prey to damaging influences. A facile, over-tolerant multiculturalism is one such; it becomes in fact another name for relativism. It follows that Europe should stand firm in defense of its values, within which unequivocal Christian teaching has a central place.[8]

Not everyone will agree with this analysis, which tips all too easily into the notion of fortress Europe: boundaries of all kinds—geographical, demographic, religious, and philosophical—must be defended. Nor do all commentators accept the argument that the Muslim constituency will necessarily grow exponentially as the European population shrinks. Apart from anything else, such remarks depend entirely on all other things being equal—which they rarely are. They depend, moreover, on the choices of women, a section of the population that have not so far been the focus of the discussion. It is now time to remedy that point.

Transcending Difference: The Role of Women

Women are more religious than men. Indeed, for Christians in the West, the difference between men and women with respect to their religious lives has become one of the most pervasive findings in the literature.[9] It shows on almost every indicator (practice, belief, self-identification, private prayer, etc.), and is found in almost every denomination—large or small, traditional or innovative, Orthodox, Catholic, or Protestant. It exists, moreover, on both sides of the Atlantic: here similarity is far more important than difference. Early reviews of this literature can be found in Francis (1997) and Walter and Davie (1998); a more recent summary is contained in Woolever et al. (2006). All three make reference to the available data. Indeed the significance of gender is a point on which almost every commentator agrees, whether their approach be quantitative (the hardest of hard statistics) or qualitative (the most impressionistic of religious sources). It is equally true for those forms of religion which appear on first reading to be hostile to the welfare of women, including fundamentalism.

Two questions immediately present themselves: why is this so and—equally importantly—why was the difference ignored for so long? For such it was, a fact that becomes increasingly difficult for students to grasp given the preoccupations of those currently engaged in the field. Here in fact is a timely and very positive example of the discipline catching up with reality. But why did it take so long? There are two rather different reasons for the delay: the first can be found in the churches themselves, the second in the limitations of social science. Within the churches—or more precisely within significant sections of the Protestant churches—a major debate about leadership took place in the second half of the twentieth century. Central to this debate was the possibility, or otherwise, that women should become ordained priests or ministers, assuming thereby the full responsibilities of leadership. The debate itself is interesting, but is not the primary point of this section. This lies in the fact that a strong focus on leadership led to a relative lack of attention regarding the place of women in the pews—not only in the Protestant churches themselves, but in the much larger Catholic constituency which (like the Orthodox) remained immune to the possibility of change regarding the priesthood. Only gradually did the pendulum begin to swing revealing disproportionate numbers of women in practically all Christian churches in the West, not only now but in the past. Historians just as much as sociologists began to adjust their spectacles.

The second reason for the delay can be found in the theoretical frameworks of social science, more precisely in the concept of patriarchy. On some readings of the sociological agenda, women of all people should be leaving the churches, given that it is the teaching of these "patriarchal" institutions that has not only disadvantaged the women who have remained within the fold, but—much more insidiously—has legitimated their subordination throughout society. Women even more than men, it follows, should be anxious to jump ship. Awkwardly for the protagonists of these theories, the data suggested something different—that men were leaving faster than women. The evidence, moreover, is cumulative: in enquiry after enquiry, the predominance of women is not only affirmed, but striking. In the short term, however, it was easier to ignore the topic than to rethink the theories.

Happily, the data triumphed. So much so that the number of articles addressing the question of *why* women are or appear to be more religious than men grows year on year—articles which engage the issue in a variety of ways. By and large these can be divided into two groups (Walter and Davie 1998): those that explain the differences between the religious behavior of men and women in terms of "nature" and those that favor explanations based on "nurture"—that is, on the different roles that men and women perform in society and, it follows, the different patterns of socialization associated with these roles. Is it the case, in other words, that women are more religious than men because of what they are, or because of what they do?

Important implications follow. They can be found first in the possibility that women are, or think themselves to be, more vulnerable than men—whether economically, socially, or physically. Religion, it follows, is a compensator, an answer to a problem that in some respects at least is specific to women. The logic of this argument demands, however, a supplementary question. Is the position of women changing in modern societies and in ways that overcome these difficulties or will the latter—despite the best efforts of the equal-opportunities lobbies—persist? One aspect of this debate is frequently referred to (De Vaus 1984; De Vaus and McAllister 1987; Becker and Hofmeister 2001) and concerns the increasing tendency for women to participate in the labor force on an equal footing with men. Paid employment not only reduces economic dependence but at the same time distracts women from their domestic responsibilities, and within this from their primary role as the bearers and carers of children. It is the latter tasks that are most closely associated with stronger indices of religious activity—hence the connection with falling birth rates. Indeed a whole series of factors need to be kept in mind at this point: the role of women in childrearing, the ways in which this has changed in recent decades, new opportunities in the labor force and the reordering of women's lives in consequence.

Broadly speaking, two ways of thinking emerge. The first argues that the roles of women have changed very significantly in the twentieth century, leading to a corresponding reduction in their need for religion—a conclusion favored very largely by European secularization theorists. Callum Brown (2000) exemplifies this point of view. Indeed Brown rests his entire account of *The Death of Christian Britain* on the transformation of gender roles that took place in the 1960s. Not only have women ceased to be noticeably more religious than men, they have ceased dramatically to fulfill their traditional function of handing on the faith to the next generation—hence, from the point of view of the churches, the extreme seriousness of this situation. Brown's book is a longitudinal study of Britain rather than Europe, but his point—if correct—still holds: the family, and that means women, is no longer fulfilling its role as the transmitters of Christian memory. It is this that preoccupies the Catholic hierarchy in Europe, and with some justification.

There are others, however, who take a different view, arguing that something much more profound is at stake in the religiousness of men and women than has been indicated so far. A differential need for religion is embedded in the personalities of male and female and is, therefore, unlikely to change in the foreseeable future, if at all. Here, in other words, is an argument based on nature rather than nurture. Interestingly, the American rational choice theorists are at least hinting that this might be the case. Recent applications of rational choice theory, for example, include a gender dimension, resting their argument on the notion that women are more risk averse than men. More precisely, it is the risk-taking aptitudes of men that permit them, relatively speaking, to live without religion—or, in terms of the theory, to make different "rational" choices (Miller and Stark 2002; Stark 2002). If this is the case, it follows that women will not only continue to be more religious than men, they will continue to "hand on" this trait to their daughters.

It is unwise, in my view, to dichotomize these choices: this is a both/and rather than either/or situation. Societies, moreover, continue to evolve. Childbearing, for example, has become not only safer but more efficient in the Western world—relatively few years are now spent in pregnancy and childrearing, leaving more time for employment within a life-span that is getting longer rather than shorter. But precisely this (a significant increase in longevity) is creating new burdens for women as they become, or more accurately remain, the primary carers of elderly people, whether in the home or in an institution (a major finding of the WREP study outlined in the previous chapter). It echoes in fact a point made by Walter and Davie at an earlier stage: namely, that it is important to look at the nature or type of women's employment as well as the fact that increasing numbers of women are now engaged in the labor force. One very obvious example can be found in the disproportionate numbers of women in the relatively low-paid service sector, in which the care of the very young and the very old remains a noticeable and persistent feature. It is, surely, an extension rather than a negation of the traditional female role.

One further contribution to the literature on gender is worth noting before closing this discussion. It can be found in Woodhead's short but very careful analyses of the contrasting ways in which different groups of women engage with religion in different parts of the world (Woodhead 2000; 2002). Rejecting the possibility that religion is necessarily a "good" or a "bad" thing for women, Woodhead emphasizes the fact that women, just like men, are very diverse; so too are the societies of which they are part. With this in mind, she looks first at the societies of the modern West, noting in particular the distinction between the private and the public sphere. Broadly speaking, women who remain in the private sphere (in the home) find it easier to affirm their religiousness than those who straddle both public and private. Such a conclusion echoes the labor-force argument cited above.

In the less developed parts of the world, however, the process of differentiation is, and always has been, less marked. Here, women have found both in religious teaching and in religious organizations a space to develop their talents, in public as well as in private. For them, religion becomes a resource, a way forward—a way moreover to curb the excesses of their menfolk, and to develop the habits that are necessary for stability or even modest improvement in parts of the world where welfare in any developed sense is lacking. A telling example can be found in the Pentecostal communities of Latin America (Martin 2000). Hence the emphatic conclusion of both Woodhead and Martin: no one should doubt the significance of gender to the sociological study of religion, but the ways that this is worked out by different groups of women, in different religious traditions, and in different parts of the world are necessarily diverse.

Such a statement provides a link to the complex issues that surround the place of women in the religious minorities now present in both Europe and the United States. These are many and varied and cannot be engaged in the detail that they deserve. Suffice it to say that disputes about the status and role of women are increasingly likely in societies which are religiously plural. They stem, moreover, from an in-built contradiction: sooner or later, even the most sensitive supporters of multiculturalism will come into conflict with the advocates of gender equality. Communities that are male-dominated and even modestly self-regulating are almost certain to violate the gender-related norms of Western society. There is a difference, however, between violating norms and breaking the law.

Few people would dispute, for instance, that arranged marriages, female circumcision, and honor killings are beyond the rule of law and cannot be tolerated in a modern democracy. Those who do these things must be punished, severely so. Rather more difficult, however, are the in-between cases, including the Muslim veil. Here, to put it mildly, there is more room for discussion. On the one hand are those for whom questions of clothing, including the veil, are simply a private matter; much more apprehensive are the commentators who see in the veil (and what it symbolizes), the thin end of an inevitably dangerous wedge.

Either way, the veil has become a potent symbol—the touchstone of vehement and ongoing debate. In some places, most notably France, the logic is inexorable: if religion is proscribed from the public sphere, the veil—as a symbol of religion—can no longer be permitted, even if this means banning the cross and the yarmulke as well. But quite apart from its place, or non-place, in public life, the veil diminishes the status of women. It is a symbol of oppression, out of place in a modern, gender-equal society. Elsewhere, the debate is more nuanced. The veil in itself is harmless; the problem lies in its imposition on those who prefer not to wear it. Yet others, including some Europeans, appropriate the veil very differently: for them, it is a fashion accessory—not only symbolic but stylish—and as varied as the groups who wear it. Take a look, for example, at the Muslim women in the African American communities; here, as indeed in many other places, it would be hard to argue that the covering of the head is in any way a negation of beauty. Quite the opposite in fact.

Who though, should decide for whom in these increasingly intense discussions? The answer must lie, surely, with the women themselves. In a mature democracy, no woman should be obliged to wear the veil against her will: that is clear. But no woman, equally, should be prevented from wearing the veil if she wishes to do so, still less by a man. And to return to a point made earlier (p. 104): many secular liberals have a better grasp of one than the other, revealing, once again, a marked lack of reciprocity in the argument.

Age, Gender, Generation, and the Life-Cycle

The reluctance of some social scientists to relate gender to religion has been discussed in some detail. The question of age is rather different. This was a shift driven by the demographic changes that were taking place in industrial societies in the late twentieth century and their likely impact on existing societal structures. The issue has already been addressed in relation to welfare. With respect to religion, practitioners of social science have fewer problems; here the age variable produces distinctive, but entirely predictable patterns (Davie and Vincent 1998). Older people are more religious than the young on all the conventional indicators, a fact that interacts with gender to produce a preponderance of older women in almost every denomination or congregation in both Europe and the United States. So much so that this is sometimes seen as a "problem." Institutions which perform admirably on important indices of inclusion (gender and age) are regarded as failures in many Western societies. In a word, they have little to do with the mainstream.

How, though, should age-related religion be understood? The literature reveals two possibilities: on the one hand, explanations which relate to the life-cycle, on the other, ways of thinking which reflect the notion of generation or cohort. The first is straightforward and rests on the premise that the closer an individual comes to death, the greater the concern with matters of mortality and therefore with the issues that, in most societies, come under the rubric of religion. The second is rather different and underlines the markedly different outlooks of the age-cohorts or generations which are found in any society. In Europe, an obvious and very important example can be found in the generations born before or after World War II. More recently, the epithets "baby boomers" and "generation X" (or Y) pervade both popular parlance and social science, not to mention the influential jargon of marketing specialists. Generations, moreover, are as different in their religious lives as they are in everything else. Hence the analysis of Callum Brown (see above), which rests on the fact that the generation of women that grew up in the 1960s no longer engaged with religion in the same way as their mothers or grandmothers. If Brown is right, the current preponderance of older women in the churches will be a temporary rather than permanent feature. The "cohort" is unlikely to be replaced.

That, however, is not the whole story. The debate that relates different patterns of religiousness to different generational outlooks must itself be placed in a broader context. More precisely, it must take account of the fact that the life-cycle as a whole is changing and in ways that have important implications for religion. Three "moments" in this process will be used as examples, in a discussion that brings together not only the themes of this variation, but of those which preceded it. Indeed in many ways, these illustrations gather up the threads that lie across as well as within these essays. The first looks at a cluster of variables surrounding childbirth, infant mortality, and baptism; the second at the prolongation of adolescence in modern societies; the third will return to old age itself.

The decline in infant mortality is an index of modernization in itself. The particular combinations of improved economic conditions and medical advance that brought this about are crucially important in historical terms. As such, however, they are not the focus of this discussion which will concentrate on a specific, but revealing issue: that is the implications of these changes for the understanding of baptism, the rite of passage associated with the birth of a new child. In this connection, the role of the historic churches as the effective registrars of birth and death through much of European history is central; it is a point already noted (Chapter 3, note 2). This, of course, is no longer the case—a change brought about for different reasons. Among them are the following: the process of institutional separation which has produced a professional class trained to deal with the registration of citizens at various points in their lives (a classic illustration of secularization); the mutation in the religious life of European societies best described as a shift from obligation to consumption (and its consequences for membership); and, thirdly, a change in the "status" of the new-born child (in the sense that an infant, who is almost certain to live to maturity, is less in need of divine blessing in either the short or the longer term). Taken together these factors have transformed the rite of baptism in the course of the twentieth century—a point with considerable implications for both sociological and theological study, including comparative work.

It becomes immediately clear, for example, that it is simply not possible to compare baptism figures across both time and place in Europe without an awareness that you might not be comparing like with like—a point underlined by Bernice Martin in her trenchant critique of social-scientific method (2003).[10] Here too can be found what David Martin calls an "angle of eschatological tension". When the gap between the historical legacy and the present realities of religious life becomes too large, something has to give. Liturgies alter to fit new situations; theologies follow suit. In other words, the rite of baptism is seen increasingly as an initiation into a voluntarist organization rather than a badge of national identity (Martin 1996: 81). Such transitions, however, are easier said than done. The pain involved in these adaptations is considerable, the more so if populations used to welcome from their churches begin to experience rejection. They are understandably bewildered when what was once enjoined becomes increasingly conditional—offered only to those who meet seemingly arbitrary conditions.

Not all European societies, however, have gone down this route—a fact that reflects persistent differences within the continent. The Church of England, for example, has seen a dramatic decline in its figures for baptism, brought about for a variety of reasons, including—it must be said—its own shifts in policy;[11] equally sharp are the falls in the Catholic Church in France. The same thing has not happened in the Lutheran churches of northern Europe. Indeed the rates of baptism in the Nordic churches remain extraordinarily high for specifically Nordic reasons—exactly the same reasons, in fact, that encourage Nordic people to pay substantial amounts of tax to their churches despite the fact that they rarely attend. Membership of the national church, denoted by baptism, remains despite everything a central plank of Nordic identity. Even more crucial for this discussion, however, is the fact that the American churches have, very largely, avoided this debate altogether. Churches that have been voluntarist from the outset have not had to engage what for many European institutions has been a necessary, difficult, and at times very painful transition. Indeed, it is hardly an exaggeration to suggest that the difficulties surrounding the rite of Christian initiation in some European churches illustrate more clearly than anything else the essential difference between the religious institutions of Europe and those in the United States.

Confirmation is somewhat similar. In most Christian traditions, moreover, it is the rite associated with adolescence. Once again, the Church of England offers a telling illustration. In England, confirmation is no longer a teenage rite of passage imposed by the institution, but a relatively rare event undertaken as a matter of personal choice by people of all ages. Hence the marked rise in the proportion of adult confirmations amongst the candidates overall. Confirmation becomes, therefore, a very significant moment for those individuals who choose this option—an attitude that is bound to effect the rite itself, which now includes the space for a public declaration of faith. It is increasingly common, moreover, to baptize an adult candidate immediately before confirmation, a gesture which is evidence in itself of the fall in infant baptism some twenty to thirty years earlier. Taken together these changes reflect an evident mutation in the nature of membership in the historic church of this country—a central theme in this discussion.

The debate, however, needs to be set in a wider context in the sense that adolescence itself is changing in nature. No longer is it a relatively brief period of transition between childhood and becoming an adult, marked for a man by getting a job, and for a woman by a move from her father's household to that of her husband. It has become instead a prolonged period for both men and women, associated (at least for some) with an extended period of education, a somewhat piecemeal entry into the labor market, and a tendency to delay marriage and childbearing until a much later stage (a point already observed). Almost everything in fact is different, including attitudes to religion. What at one stage was a brief and somewhat rebellious transition is now almost a way of life.

With this in mind, two bodies of empirical data are worth noting, one European and one American. The most recent findings of the European Values Study have provoked comment in this respect.[12] Unsurprisingly, the data demonstrate unequivocally that younger generations in Europe are markedly less religious than the old in terms of the more conventional religious indicators. That was expected. More intriguingly, today's adolescents are rather more likely than their predecessors to experiment with innovative forms of religion. Here, more specifically, is a generation disproportionately attracted to the idea of an immanent God (a "God in me") and to the conviction that there is some sort of "life after death." The shift, moreover, is most evident in the parts of Europe where the historic churches are relatively weak—in other words in societies where two things are happening at once. On the one hand, traditional disciplines have broken down; conventional forms of religious transmission, it follows, are unlikely to take place (Fulton et al. 2000). Equally important, however, is the freedom that emerges once this rupture has occurred; it leads, it seems, to experimentation with new forms of religion as much as to rejection.[13]

In terms of the United States, the findings from the National Study of Youth and Religion (NSYR) offer an interesting comparison (Smith 2005). The data for this enquiry are taken from a nationwide telephone survey of American teenagers and their parents, followed by a series of in-depth face-to-face interviews with more than 250 of the survey respondents. Here, for a start, is a study larger and more detailed than is possible in most of Europe. Its results are interesting. Religion emerges as a significant factor in the lives of many American teenagers. Teenagers, moreover, are far more influenced by the religious beliefs and practices of their parents and other adults than was commonly thought; they are not, conversely, the "spiritual seekers" so often assumed in the literature and hinted at in the recent data from the European Values Study. What emerges in fact is a paradox. Religion is widely practiced and positively valued by American teenagers; it is also associated with positive rather than negative behavior. At the same time, religion is poorly understood by the great majority of those contacted through this project. Indeed, the authors go so far as to suggest a major transformation in the United States, away from the substantive teaching of historical religious traditions and toward a new and quite different outlook, which they call a "Moralistic Therapeutic Deism." MTD is a benign and relatively undemanding form of Christianity, noticeably content-light. Here perhaps is a teenage form of Ammerman's "golden-rule" Christianity described in Chapter 4.

Even this, however, is qualitatively different from Europe. Substantial numbers of American teenagers continue to attend their churches; that is not so in Europe. American foundations, moreover, are prepared to invest very considerable sums of money in researching this situation. Hence the aims of the NSYR, clearly set out on the project website. They are revealing in themselves:

> To research the shape and influence of religion and spirituality in the lives of American youth; to identify effective practices in the religious, moral, and

social formation of the lives of youth; to describe the extent and perceived effectiveness of the programs and opportunities that religious communities are offering to their youth; and to foster an informed national discussion about the influence of religion in youth's lives, in order to encourage sustained reflection about and rethinking of our cultural and institutional practices with regard to youth and religion.[14]

The policy implications are abundantly clear—they are worth noting in a country in which, for the constitutional reasons already explained, there is no religious education in the public school system.

The third illustration returns to old age itself, setting this within the context of increased longevity in all developed societies—a fact of considerable significance for the churches. The issues can be looked at from a variety of perspectives. The first is entirely positive: religious organizations cope well with older people and are expected to do so (a conclusion firmly endorsed by the WREP study and likely to continue for some time). Indeed for significant sections of the elderly populations of Europe, notably women and those who live in rural areas, the churches constitute the only effective network. Equally affirming is the growing body of data on both sides of the Atlantic which establish a link between religious activity, variously defined, and the prolongation of life (see for example Levin 1994; Koenig, Larson, and Matthews 1996; Cohen and Koenig 2003; Flannelly, Weaver, Larson, and Koenig 2002). The connections may be direct or indirect, in the sense that religious commitment (prayer, bible reading, fellowship, and so on) may be good in themselves, but at the same time they encourage life styles that are conducive to healthy living. Either way, the religiously active are happier, healthier, and live longer— achievements that most people would view positively.

Beneath these common qualities can be found, however, a noticeable difference between Europe and the United States. What in Europe have become in many cases the institutions of older people can, in the much freer market of the United States, be differently configured: here have emerged institutions not *of,* but *for,* older people. In Europe, older people are the residual category: those who are left when younger generations are no longer attracted to the organizations in question. In the United States, seniors—just like young people—become a slice of the market that is well worth competing for. The contrast should not be exaggerated: there is merit in both models—in the social care of the parish extended to all those who live within its borders, and in the specialist organizations emerging to pastor particular sections of the population. The subtext, however, is noticeably different; so too are the possible futures. In Europe, this generation may be the last to move through the life-cycle as defined, and marked by the churches; in the United States this is less likely to be the case.

That said, it is important not to jump to conclusions. Almost all Europeans continue to touch base with their churches at the time of a death. Or to put the same point in a different way, it is perfectly possible in most European societies to have a secular funeral, but not that many people do so. Why not gives pause for thought. Such reflections return us to a tension set out in Variation One: that is the notion of two economies running side by side in the traditional churches of Europe (p. 41). Interestingly, exactly the same tension can be considered with reference to the life-course, a perspective that fits well within the argument of this chapter—as follows. The first, and still emerging, economy relates to the model of choice. Church membership is reserved for those with approved religious convictions and, where appropriate, for their children as well. It is precisely these sentiments that are, bit by bit, bringing about changes in both the practice and theologies of baptism, though more in some places than in others.[15] The second, and much older, economy can be seen at the time of a death. It is at this point, if no other, that the historic churches of Europe are open to all, and are likely to remain so for the foreseeable future. Here, in fact, is the very essence of vicarious religion: a notion that captures both the care of the churches for their "people," and the expectations of European populations that this will be so.

For American readers, one episode can be used to display the notion of vicarious religions better than almost any other: it concerns moreover their function at the time of a death—the death in this case of Princess Diana. Like many English people of her class and generation, Diana was baptized and nurtured in the Church of England, where her marriage to Prince Charles took place. As her marriage began to collapse, Diana sought solace in a number of places, including alternative forms of spirituality—a side of her nature to which the public readily responded. Diana's "self" and evident mortality found expression in the laying of flowers, the lighting of candles, and the signing of books. Any element of judgment, conversely, was noticeable by its absence. Also set on one side was the fact that, when she died, Princess Diana was keeping company with the son of a prominent Muslim. It was, it seems, axiomatic that her funeral should take place in the same church in which her public life began, Westminster Abbey, and more privately at her home in Northamptonshire, a decision quite clearly endorsed by the population as a whole. Had the Dean of Westminster Abbey refused this privilege, the strength of the reaction can only be imagined (Davie and Martin 1999).

Gathering the Threads

What can be said in conclusion? This variation has considered in some detail the interrelationships between religion and four very different indicators of social difference. Reference has also been made to the political implications of the first two of these (class and ethnicity), and to the significance of the last three (ethnicity, gender, and generation) for the handing on of the religious tradition or memory within the family. The latter function, it is important to remember, must be set against the changing nature of the family itself. No longer is it necessarily the norm that a child grows up with the same two parents for most of his or her childhood. Divorce rates are high in both the United States and Europe, single parents exist in large numbers, and households are regularly reconstituted. At the same time, same-sex partnerships are becoming more and more frequent—though not always recognized in law, still less by the churches. This last has become a highly contentious issue.

What, then, is similar and what is different between Europe and the United States in the handing on of the religious tradition? It is clear, first of all, that gender remains a crucial variable on both sides of the Atlantic: it is women who do a great deal of the "work." Equally important are generational shifts, though their impact is somewhat different: young people in America remain churchgoers to an extent that is seldom found in Europe, though exactly what this means in terms of theological understanding is more difficult to say. Newly arrived populations, finally, find particular ways of passing on their distinctive identities. There is some evidence that the recently arrived increase their religious activity to conform to the norm in the United States. It would be tempting to say that the reverse is the case in Europe, but this is not entirely true. What religious minorities—and most notably Islam—have achieved in Europe is a reassertion of the place of religion in public life and, as part and parcel of this, a resistance to at least some of the changes in family structure indicated above. The point is nicely illustrated in the requirements set for those arriving in the Netherlands, where permissive attitudes are at their most developed. Beneath these "tests" lies a strong subtext: if you do not like what is now taken for granted in Dutch society, it would be better if you lived elsewhere. To what extent such views are consonant with the tolerance so highly prized in this long-standing and in many ways very advanced democracy constitutes an ongoing and sociologically very intriguing question.

Notes

1   Learning to see, identify and interpret the physical presence of such churches should be part of any course in social scientific method. A great deal of information can be gleaned by careful looking.

2   To some extent this is a Protestant–Catholic distinction. The discipline of mass attendance in Catholicism most certainly makes a difference.

3   Afro-Caribbeans were not made welcome in the mainstream churches of Britain. As a result they set up independent Afro-Caribbean churches, now some of the most vibrant religious communities in urban Britain. Even more recent (i.e. after 2004)—and totally unexpected—is the arrival in both the United Kingdom and Ireland of large numbers of Poles, many of whom are practicing Catholics.

4   The following list should be regarded as indicative rather than exhaustive. Nielsen (2004) contains an extensive and very useful bibliographic essay on Islam in Europe. More recent references include Cesari (2004), Fetzer and Soper (2004), Cesari and McLoughlin (2005), Klausen (2005), Buruma (2006), Byrnes and Katzenstein (2006), Al-Azmeh and Fokas (2007) and Jenkins (2007).

5   Casanova's chapter is published in Banchoff (2007), which brings together a series of papers on democracy and new forms of religious pluralism in both Europe and the United States. The comparative dimension is central to this publication.

6   See, for example, Haddad and Smith (1993), Smith (1999), Esposito et al. (2004) and Geaves et al. (2004).

7   See in particular the Pluralism Project at Harvard, the Prince Alwaleed Bin Talal Center for Muslim–Christian Understanding at Georgetown University, and the MacDonald Center for the Study of Islam and Christian Muslin Relations at Hartford Seminary. The last of these is interesting: a seminary established to train missionaries to work in the Muslim world has now become a center for dialogue and mutual understanding.

8   The central importance of Christian values has been reinforced by a yet more surprising collaboration—that between Benedict XVI and Jürgen Habermas. In *The Dialectics of Secularization: On Reason and Religion* (Habermas and Ratzinger 2006), the "methodological atheist" and the current Pope question the possibility that secular reason provides sufficient grounds for a democratic constitutional state.

9   It is important to remember that such statements refer only to Christianity. Generalization to other world faiths should be avoided.

10 A point of view challenged in turn by David Voas in his painstaking work on religious demography (Voas 2003a; 2003b).

11 Church of England parishes have adopted very different policies in this respect: some baptize all children brought to them; some set more or less strict conditions of those who ask for the rite (attendance by the family for so many weeks, for example); others restrict the rite only to active church members. The

piecemeal nature of these changes contributes considerably to the resentments felt by the population. For the outsider, the logic is very hard to discern.

12 The European Values Study is a large-scale, cross-national, and longitudinal survey research program concerned with basic human values, initiated by the European Value Systems Study Group (EVSSG) in the late 1970s. There have been three waves of the survey to date: in 1981, 1990, and 1999/2000. The first survey included 15 countries, the second 32, and the third, 33 (though not all countries surveyed are European: the United States and Canada for example were included in the first two surveys). More details can be found on the regularly updated website: http://www.europeanvalues.nl/index2.htm (accessed 6 May 2008). Regarding young people in particular, see Bréchon (2001) and Lambert (2002).

13 That said, a recent study of young people in Britain found that "Generation Y" (i.e. those born since 1982) were very largely indifferent to religion—there was little sign of experimentation here (Savage et al. 2006).

14 See the regularly updated NSYR website both for these aims and for the continuing development of this project: http://www.youthandreligion.org/research/ (accessed 6 May 2008).

15 The point should not be exaggerated. These changes are most noticeable in parts of northern Europe: the United Kingdom, the Netherlands, France, and to some extent in Germany. The Nordic churches are more resistant for the reasons already given. In southern Europe the traditional patterns very largely endure; this is also the case in the Orthodox countries.

Chapter 7

So What? Policy Implications[1]

Social scientists do not take an oath promising to be practically useful. There is the famous case of a British association of mathematicians which, reputedly, continues to open its regular meetings with a toast: "To pure mathematics, and may it never be of use to anyone!" There is no compelling moral argument why some social scientists may not indulge in a comparable sentiment. And, indeed, some of us, when asked why we pursue this or that topic, may reply, "Because it interests me" or, in moments of frankness, "Because I want to shoot out of the water the theory of Professor X— I hate his guts." Nevertheless, most of us like to think, with good reason, that our intellectual endeavors can be useful to various purposes in which we believe—to ameliorate this or that deplorable situation in our own or some other society, to help a movement whose agenda we share, and, last but not least, to influence public opinion and the policies of our respective governments. The considerations of this book lend themselves particularly to the last of these purposes. It makes sense, then, to conclude these considerations with an attempt to answer the question "So what?" Specifically, what are the implications of the comparison of religion in the United States and Europe for public opinion on both sides of the Atlantic, and for the policies of governments on the two continents?

Rather more prosaically, relations between the United States and Europe have reached a certain low point. They have not improved in the time that it has taken to complete this book. There are several reasons for this: some are based on the actions of governments, others on slower processes of cultural divergence. Clearly, the role of religion is an important fact as one compares the two cultures. It follows that the present topic, while it obviously relates to theoretical speculation, has in addition some robustly practical implications.

The argument will unfold as follows. It will deal first with the very different place of religion in both Europe and the United States—bringing together the material from the previous chapters. It will then work out the consequence of these differences—first for domestic policy, then for foreign policy, and then for what is in many ways the crucial question: the vexed relationship between Europe and the United States and the place of religion in this. All three, however, lead to further questions. How can we understand these things better and what theoretical tools might be necessary in order to do this? Rejoining the narrative at the end of Variation Two (pp. 63–4)—itself predicated on the differences between the European and the American Enlightenments—the chapter concludes first by re-engaging the notion of multiple modernities (thereby placing both Europe and the United States in a global context) and then by examining the implications for the social-scientific agenda. Where—if pursued to its logical conclusions—does this material lead us in terms of social-scientific thinking? "Into new territory" is the honest answer.

Mutual perceptions are influenced by (typically pejorative) stereotypes—the starting point of much of our thinking. In Europe, there is the perception of the United States as a country dominated by religious fanatics with irrational views on abortion and the death penalty and with a penchant for invading countries on a millenarian mission to remake the world in America's image. In the United States, Europe is widely perceived as a decadent civilization steeped in atheism and hedonism, headed for extinction due to its unwillingness to defend itself militarily and its even more ominous reluctance to have children; given the latter two alleged facts, there is the notion that the future will see the continent becoming "Eurabia." The policies (real or perceived) of the current Bush administration have clearly added to such European perceptions of the United States, and European reactions to these policies have stimulated anti-European feelings among Americans. The cultural divergences, however, go much deeper than the disagreements of the last few years.

Stereotypes color our thinking; they also contain some elements of truth. It is true, for example, that religion plays a political role in the United States which would be inconceivable in Europe; it is also true that the hegemonic power of the United States has led to military interventions that European governments would be much less willing (or indeed able) to undertake. It is true, vide the preceding chapters of this book, that almost all religious indicators are much more feeble in western and central Europe than they are in the United States, that the European model of the welfare state has led to very high expectations of material comfort as a civic entitlement, and that the demographic trajectory in Europe is likely to lead to very serious problems for the welfare model as this is currently envisaged.

Yet, as soon as one looks closely at the empirical situation—examined at length in each of our variations—it becomes clear that the stereotypes are as much false as true: the situation on both sides of the Atlantic is much more complicated. The United States, for example, is not as religious as it seems. More precisely, there is a "culture war" going on between a highly secularized cultural elite and a strongly religious populace; the religious rhetoric of the Bush administration is nothing new but stands in a long tradition shaped by both Puritanism and the American Enlightenment; and recent military adventures of the United States have been motivated (rightly or wrongly) by strategic considerations that have little if anything to do with religious ideas. One may add that the idea of democracy being carried on the tip of bayonets (admittedly an idea influencing current American policies in the Middle East) is based, not on the Puritan heritage, but on a decidedly European, indeed French, doctrine—its classical name was Jacobinism and its most famous protagonist was that well-known born-again Christian Napoleon Bonaparte. As to the complimentary set of stereotypes on the other side of the Atlantic, Europe is not as secular as it seems; some European governments (with the United Kingdom in the lead, from the Falklands to Iraq) have been quite willing to use military means for certain policy ends; and—finally—it is very unclear that there is any direct linkage between low religious indicators and low birth rates.

Pejorative stereotypes, moreover, are not only intellectually sloppy, they are politically harmful—given that they influence, directly and indirectly, our attitudes to the modern world order, which continues to evolve. During the cold war, for example, the United States and Europe identified themselves self-consciously as "the West" in opposition to the communist threat. Since the demise of the Soviet empire, that threat has virtually disappeared (though it would be unwise to assume that it may not reappear in new forms). There are, however, other threats which affect both continents: these include radical Islamism (most immediately), an imperially minded Chinese superpower (more tentatively), and a series of anti-democratic movements in various developing societies (perhaps more violently). But quite apart from new threats, there are other reasons for proposing that "the West" is not an obsolete concept. More than any other two world regions, the United States and Europe share common values of human rights, the rule of law, and democracy; they also share (with whatever variations) the political institutions by which these values can be realized. If one assents to these values, one must hope that the current tensions between the two will diminish and that, consequently, there will be a higher degree of cooperation on various international issues. Of course this will not be achieved simply by reducing misperceptions in the matter of religion. But such reduction can be helpful—a principal goal of the present volume.

The implications of thinking in these terms for both domestic and foreign policy are many and varied and will be taken in turn. Two points, however, must be underlined before embarking on the enterprise. The first is to appreciate that the comparison is necessarily imbalanced: the United States is one country, Europe is not and contains within itself a huge variety of solutions, or non-solutions, to the resurgence of religion in public life. The present situation in Europe, moreover, is paradoxical: the reassertion of religious issues is taking place alongside a continuing erosion of traditional religious practices and the forms of behavior that go with these. It is precisely this combination that provokes unease. It reveals, in fact, a second contrast between the two cases—one that has emerged in almost all of our variations. In the United States, religion is seen as a resource (the means by which to resolve secular as well as religious dilemmas); in Europe, it is part of the problem—the more so, whether fairly or not, with reference to Islam. Either way, the implications for policy-making are considerable.

Dealing with Religion at Home

The public role of religion in America is particularly visible in domestic politics. Examples abound in the previous chapters, only some of which need recalling here. Almost all of them begin from the ongoing debate concerning the precise meaning of the separation of church and state as enshrined in the First Amendment (a theme developed in Variation Three). Broadly speaking, one set of protagonists argue that the establishment clause is there precisely to safeguard its free-exercise provision—the state must not favor any one religion, so as to allow freedom for all. Those on the other side, however—while definitely endorsing the free exercise in the sense of religious freedom for all—insist that no-establishment means that religion must have no place at all in any public space related to government. One may call these two views, respectively, the soft and the hard version of separation. Historians mostly agree that the original intent of the framers of the amendment was on the soft side, while the hard version is of more recent origin.

The disagreement relates in turn to two rather different views of the constitution itself, with conservatives insisting that the courts must be bound by the original intent of whatever part of the constitution they apply, while liberals think of the constitution as not a fixed text but an organic one, spouting new applications as time changes. This disagreement about the application of the constitution has become a defining issue between the two sides of the political spectrum in American politics, on many issues that have nothing to do with religion. But religion has become enmeshed in this controversy, with far-reaching political consequences. Understandably, people with conservative religious views—Protestants, Catholics, and Jews—have gravitated to the conservative view, which is or seems to be more friendly to religion, and consequently to the Republican party which has upheld this view.

Indeed, the conservative movement of the last half-century was originally triggered by a Supreme Court decision affecting religion and based on a liberal view of the constitution—that is the 1963 ruling that prayer in public schools was unconstitutional. Many religious Americans felt that this decision meant that their faith was denigrated and that they themselves were marginalized in the public life of the country. Ten years later came the Supreme Court decision declaring abortion to be a constitutional right (based on the liberal idea that a right to privacy was implied by the constitution though no such right is mentioned there). This, as we have seen, was regarded by some as a solemn ratification of a moral evil. Not only did it further galvanize the conservative movement; at the same time, it attracted large numbers of conservative Protestants/ Evangelicals and Catholics to the Republican party. Somewhat later, other so-called "social issues," relating to feminism and the gay movement, were drawn into the same cultural and political divide. Thus, when the sociologist James Hunter published a book in 1991 entitled *Culture Wars: The Struggle to Define America*, the thesis contained in the title gained immediate plausibility. Interestingly, to European ears the phrase "culture war" (usually employed in the singular) has a suggestive undertone—it almost exactly translates the term *Kulturkampf*, which was used to describe the conflict between Bismarck's government and the Catholic Church about the place of religion first in Prussia and then in the new German Reich.

Returning to America, it is important to make a distinction between the "politics" and the "culture" of these divisions. If one looks only at the politics, one gets the impression of a deeply divided country, polarized between "red" and "blue" voting blocks. Yet the really deep divisions are not between such blocks, but between two groups of highly ideological activists that, more or less accidentally, have become key constituencies of the two major parties. Political parties in a democracy require committed activists—people who can do the footwork of campaigns and, most importantly, people who write checks. In the Republican party this includes large numbers of religious conservatives, in the Democratic party large numbers of people who take the liberal side on the "social issues" and who are more secular than the general population. The political result of this fact was glaringly apparent in the 2000 and 2004 presidential elections. The single most important factor deciding whether an individual voted Republican or Democratic was—not income, not education, not gender, not age—but degree of religious commitment. Strong majorities of religious people voted for Bush, majorities of religiously less or uncommitted people voted against him. Generally speaking, the Democrats have come to be seen as unfriendly to religion, the Republicans as friendly. As the 2008 elections approach, prominent Democrats are working hard to overcome what has clearly become a disadvantage in the race for the White House.

The country, however, is much less divided culturally than its politics make it appear. Americans tend toward the center. Survey data, for example, show that on all the neuralgic "social issues," most Americans hold middle-of-the-road opinions. Thus most Americans do not like abortion, but would not want to make it illegal again—rather would impose more restrictions. Similarly most Americans do not particularly like homosexuality, but are tolerant enough toward homosexuals, and are ready to concede them all sorts of rights as long as they do not usurp the traditional meaning of marriage. But even on the issue of same-sex marriage (which a majority of Americans rejects), there is an absence of passion outside the activist groups battling this project. The dominant feeling is nicely captured by the comment of a comedian: "Same-sex marriage? Sure. Welcome to the joys of alimony!" Joking apart, these examples reveal a central paradox in current American politics, which lies in the fact that, in either party, a candidate cannot be nominated without the endorsement of the respective activists, but cannot be elected without veering back toward the middle and thus disappointing his or her original supporters. Given the nature of the American political system, it is difficult to see how this situation could change in the near future. This would require a very high degree of statesmanship which is not much in supply. Consequently, it is likely that religion will continue to be entangled in this political paradox.

What can be said about Europe? Clearly the stereotype prevailing in America about European church–state relations—militantly secular if not atheist—is also very distorted. It assumes, for example, that all of Europe adheres to the French model of *laïcité*. Even in France there are hard and soft versions of this model—a point developed in Variation Three. But quite apart from this, French *laïcité* is the exception, not the rule, in Europe—keeping in mind that Turkey, ironically, has followed the French example (see below for the multiple paradoxes that follow from this). The subtleties of these very different arrangements and their implications for policy can be illustrated in a brief comparison between Britain, more especially England, and France, which concerns the manner in which each of these societies deals with religious minorities. At the same time it reveals just how complex are the connections between tolerance and democracy—an exercise that invites comparison with the American case.

The facts and figures are already clear (pp. 101–102): France now houses the largest Muslim community in western Europe; Britain contains a much more diverse religious population. Both constitutionally and institutionally, moreover, France is undoubtedly a more democratic society. Here—as we have already seen—is a secular republic, with two elected chambers, no privileged church (in the sense of connections to the state), and a school system in which religious symbols are proscribed by law. There is a correspondingly strong stress on the equality of all citizens whatever their ethnic or religious identity. As a result, France follows a strongly assimilationist policy towards incomers, with the express intention of eradicating difference—individuals who arrive in France are welcome to maintain their religious belief and practices, provided these are kept firmly in the private sphere. They are actively discouraged from developing any kind of group identity. Exactly the same point can be put as follows: any loyalty (religious or otherwise) that comes between the citizen and the state is regarded in negative terms. In France, it follows, *communautarisme* is a pejorative word, implying a less than full commitment to the nation embodied in the French state.

Britain is very different. On a strict measure of democracy, Britain fares less well than France—with no written constitution, a monarchy, a half-reformed and so far unelected House of Lords, and an established church. More positively, Britain has a more developed tradition of accommodating group identities (including religious ones) within the framework of British society, a feature that owes a good deal to the relatively greater degree of religious pluralism that has existed in Britain for centuries rather than decades. Hence a markedly different policy towards newcomers: the goal becomes the accommodation of difference rather than its eradication. Rather more provocative, however, are the conclusions that emerge if you look carefully at who, precisely, in British society is advocating religious as opposed to ethnic toleration. Very frequently it turns out to be those in society who do not depend on an electoral mandate: the royal family and significant spokespersons in the House of Lords (where other faith communities are well represented by appointment, not by election).

They are both, of course, intimately connected to the established church, a significant player in its own right. Here the crucial point turns on a distinction frequently lost on Americans: that is the need to appreciate the difference between a historically strong state church and its modern, somewhat weaker equivalent. The former almost by definition becomes excluding and exclusive; the latter cannot. It can, however, use its still considerable influence to include rather than exclude, to acknowledge rather than to ignore, and to welcome rather than despise. Even more positive are its capacities to create and to sustain a space within society in which faith is taken seriously—doing so by means of its connections with the state. If these things are done well, it would be hard to argue that an established church has no part to play in an increasingly plural society.

This is not a question of "good" or "bad" solutions to the growing presence of different faith communities in twenty-first century Europe. Each of the models outlined above has its supporters and detractors—plus a marked tendency, especially among the latter, to imagine that the grass on the other side of the fence is likely to be greener. The comparison is none the less instructive given that it tells us a great deal about the societies in question quite apart from the religious minorities now living in them. So, too, does the German model, where no church is any longer established by the state, but where there is the legal status of "corporation of public law"—a status granted to some religious communities but not to others. The implications for education were discussed in Variation Three. The Dutch model of "pillarization" offers a fourth possibility. Here a great deal of social life has been organized along denominational lines—conservative Calvinist, liberal Calvinist, Catholic, and "humanist"—a situation which necessarily offers an opportunity to newcomers to form an institutional "column" of their own. The problems arise when the minorities in question not only do this, but assert within their pillar habits which are considered antithetical to Dutch society taken as a whole.

The list of countries could continue, each with its particular attributes, which derive very largely from the specificities of their histories, in which church–state relationships figure prominently. The crucial point, however, lies deeper. Despite the fact that these models have weakened in significance due to pervasive secularization throughout Europe, they continue to be socially and politically relevant. More than this: they very largely determine the responses of different European countries to the challenge of the new Muslim presence discovered in almost every part of the continent.

It is important to understand this challenge correctly. It is not an issue of religious freedom in the narrower sense—no European country denies the right of Muslims to believe in and to practice their religion. Rather, the issue is of the place of Islam in the public sphere. And this issue, in multiple and interesting ways, has reopened the whole question of religion in society which most Europeans had thought of as settled. Regardless of the church–state model, European secularization has imposed certain rules of the game on religious believers. These rules add up to a straightforward bargain: "You are completely free to live by your religion in private, but keep it out of the public sphere." Protestants came to accept this bargain in most countries. Jews did so with considerable enthusiasm, because it afforded them protection and opportunity. The Catholic Church resisted the bargain for a long time, and still does in theory, but by and large it has been pushed to accept it in practice. (There are exceptions, as in vigorous attempts by the church, for example in Italy and Spain, to oppose certain secularizing actions of government.) In all likelihood large numbers of Muslims in Europe are also willing to abide by this private–public dichotomy. But considerable numbers of Muslims do not, and herein lies the challenge.

This is not the place to discuss the question of whether Islam is fundamentally unable to accept the private–public dichotomy: Islam, after all, has from its beginnings been not only a faith, but a system of political and social organization. Be that as it may, there have been a number of critical points at which Muslims challenged the European bargain. Education, understandably, has been one of these (see Variation Three), but there are others as well—notably those that pertain to the public status of Islam. This raises a series of questions. Is the state to set limits to the immigration of imams, possibly excluding those with more militant views? Is the state to help train indigenous imams in Europe? What limits, if any, are to be set up for the construction of mosques? Height of minarets? Loudspeakers broadcasting the daily calls to prayer? There are also questions of civil law, especially– as we have seen—those that pertain to the status of women in marriage, property, and inheritance, where Islamic law (and Muslim mores) frequently collide with European law and culture. Some of these issues are symbolic, signaling acceptance or non-acceptance of Islam as a legitimate presence within European societies. Almost all of them touch directly on the real lives of Muslims, in some cases on their deepest aspirations (as in the education and thus the future of their children). Hence their significance and the questions they provoke. To what extent can a separate Muslim subculture be accepted? And if it is, will it or will it not undermine the social cohesion of European societies (a process known, with some justification, as "balkanization")?

All of this can be summarized metaphorically: immigration has posed problems of collective identity for quite some time. There have been liberal answers to these questions which have worked pretty well in many European countries, despite the persistence of racial prejudices. If you learn our language, obey our laws, and accept our way of life, your skin color does not matter. Welcome to Europe, or to whichever European society to which you wish to belong. But these liberal answers no longer work when there are considerable numbers of people who do not want to accommodate to a European way of life, who regard Europe as an alien, immoral society from which Muslims, even if they are European citizens, should segregate themselves. (Leave aside here the, happily small, number of Muslims who would like to destroy this society and replace it with an Islamic state.) Thus the Islamic challenge has created a problem that goes far beyond the issue of how to respond to the increasing presence of Muslims. The challenge is to European secularity and its bargain concerning religion. It raises very directly the question of European identity. Just what are European values, and how do they relate to religion in general and to Europe's Christian roots in particular? The debate over the inclusion or non-inclusion of references to religion in the proposed constitution of the European Union made this question very palpable. Equally significant is the possible accession of Turkey to the European Union, a question that convulses Europe as much as Turkey itself. It will be dealt with in the following section.

Foreign Policy

It is important first to return to the United States. The foreign policy of the United States is directly affected by religion—in general, because of the salience of religion in American public life, and specifically, because religious freedom has been designated as an important foreign-policy goal, both rhetorically and legally. Rhetorically it is part and parcel of the democratic ideology (the "American Creed," if you will) which has characterized the nation since its inception. It was, of course, dramatically reaffirmed in the second inaugural address of George W. Bush, with special emphasis on the Middle East. Leaving aside the question of whether the promotion of democracy in that part of the world is a feasible project, the policy creates serious dilemmas for the American government. These can be summed up in one simple question: given the American understanding of democracy, what is supposed to be the posture of the United States with regard to countries that define themselves in religious terms?

At the time of writing this question is most relevant in the Islamic world. Most knowledgeable analysts of that world understand that American notions of the separation of church and state cannot be readily transposed there. The current debates over the status of Islam and Islamic law in the constitution of Iraq illustrate the problem very sharply. The American government has accepted, however reluctantly, that in some sense a special place will be reserved for Islam in the Iraqi state. But will this mean a general, hopefully vague statement to the effect that legislation should be inspired by "Islamic values"? Or will it mean that the full brunt of Islamic law, the *shari'a*, will be applied—including its criminal penalties, its provisions concerning the status of women, and its denigration of non-Muslims to second-class citizens? For obvious strategic reasons, the United States has not made a serious issue of this in its relations with Saudi Arabia, a vitally important ally, while it has attacked Iran, a hostile country, on precisely the same grounds. In milder forms (at least thus far) the same problem appears in parts of the non-Muslim world—as in the debates over the status of Orthodoxy in Russia, of Judaism in Israel, and of Hinduism in India. Ideological consistency is hard to come by in the real world of international relations, and the democratic ideology of the United States is no exception to this.

But the challenge to American foreign policy is not just a matter of ideology and rhetoric. It has become a matter of law. In the late 1990s (during the Clinton administration—Bush cannot be blamed or praised for this one) Congress legislated two items: the State Department, in addition to its annual report on human rights in every country in the world, must now issue a separate report on religious freedom everywhere. Legislation also established the United States Commission on International Religious Freedom, which investigates cases of alleged violations of this freedom, assigns the label "country of concern" where it finds serious violations, and then makes recommendation to the President up to and including economic sanctions (which he is free to disregard on grounds of national interest). Both the annual reports and the actions of the commission have been criticized as being soft on American allies, but on the whole it is generally acknowledged that the facts are about right. (Leave aside the question by what right the foreign policy apparatus of one country gives grades, from A to F, to every other country on earth—a question which, understandably, has been raised with some acerbity abroad.)

Here, in fact, is another simple question: just which violations of religious freedom are deemed to be of truly serious concern? To be sure, there are clear cases—say, if adherents of a minority are massacred or expelled, or if a particular religious tradition is proscribed. But there are less clear cases. A troublesome question is that of proselytism (a term of opprobrium in many countries). Western views of religious freedom assume, not only that people have the right to believe and worship as they will, but that they also have the right to seek the conversion of others to their beliefs and practices. Precisely that latter right is challenged in a long list of countries—of course throughout the Muslim world, but also in Russia, Israel, India, and China. (In parenthesis, Greece—though a long-standing member of the European Union—falls seriously short of Western norms in this respect.) Again, it is a clear case if missionaries are slaughtered. But what if they are expelled, denied visas, or otherwise hampered in their activities? This is a special issue for Evangelicals, who regard missionary activity as a binding Christian duty. Evangelical missionaries are active throughout the world in large numbers and they will not be deterred by discouragement by their own or other governments. Some other American denominations, notably the Mormons, have similar missionary proclivities.

This leads to a more general and much debated question, which concerns both the nature and the degree of Evangelical influences on current American foreign policy. Recent material from the Pew Research

Center provide a good picture of what is going on;[2] so too does the work of Christian Smith (1998; 2000), already referred to. First off, it is important to distinguish the general attitudes of the Evangelical population from the activities of Evangelical organizations (such as the National Association of Evangelicals and the Southern Baptist Convention, the largest Evangelical denomination). Somewhat surprisingly, Evangelicals as a whole do not differ from the general population in their views on foreign policy (including the invasion of Iraq), with one crucial exception—they are more pro-Israel than any other non-Jewish group. That said, American policy in the Middle East has always been strongly pro-Israel under every administration, Republican or Democratic. With this in mind, one must be skeptical about the degree to which Evangelical sentiments have been an important factor in the policies of the Bush junior administration.

But when it comes to the activities of Evangelical organizations, there has been significant influence in three areas of foreign policy, each of these leading to different and at times surprising ad hoc alliances. With respect to human rights, for example, Evangelicals quite clearly played an important role in the two congressional actions mentioned above concerning religious freedom in different parts of the world, leading in this case to an alliance with the broader (and generally liberal) human-rights community. The second issue, the international traffic in women for sexual purposes, has also led to an Act of Congress, in which Evangelicals found rather different allies—this time in the feminist movement. Thirdly, on the issue of the civil wars in Sudan, allies were found in the Congressional Black Caucus. With respect to this example, it is important to grasp that interest in Sudan was first stimulated by the civil war in southern Sudan, where the rebels were mostly Christians, but this interest was then extended to Darfur, where the dividing line is racial rather than religious.

It is not difficult to see why these three questions should be of particular interest to committed Evangelicals. The point at issue is that each leads to a different political configuration—this is not a question of bloc voting. More precisely these data indicate a degree of sophistication in the Evangelical approach to foreign policy, not easily understandable in terms of widespread views identifying Evangelicals with the Christian Right. The latter, in fact, are somewhat more plausible in terms of domestic issues developed in the previous section, notably abortion and homosexuality, where Evangelicals have made alliances with yet another group: this time with conservative Catholics. There has been some spillover from this into foreign policy, notably in the campaign against AIDS, especially in Africa, where the Agency for International Development has been propagating sexual abstinence and fidelity over other means of prevention.

Understandably, religion does not play a comparable role in the foreign policy of Europe, with one important exception: the possible admission of Turkey to the European Union, in which the religious factor has become increasingly dominant. Both the political class and the European public now address this complex and continuing debate in religious terms. Such was not always the case. Here, in fact, is an excellent example of the shift from religion as "invisible" to religion as a stumbling block. How can we comprehend this change?

Given its strategic position between East and West, Turkey is of interest to the United States as well as to Europe. Of itself, this is nothing new. The future alignment of Turkey has however a particular resonance in the first decade of the twenty-first century, at least in part because of the growing significance of religion in global affairs. So much is clear. Much more complicated are the details of these shifting parameters. Briefly, the modern Republic of Turkey emerged in 1923 from the ruins of the Ottoman Empire. Under Kemal Atatürk, Turkey experienced a rigorous program of reform—a process of Westernization bringing with it constitutional change and an enforced secularization of public life. The nascent republic was in fact closely modeled on France: Turkey is one country where the quintessentially French notion of *laïcité* has had an immediate impact. Unsurprisingly, many of the same problems ensue—the wearing of the headscarf in public life, for example, has been as contentious in Turkey as it has been in France, despite the fact that Turkey remains a predominantly Muslim society.

Indeed the key question in Turkey—just as much as in Europe—follows from this: how can a rigorously secular state accommodate the manifestation of Islam in public as well as private life, the more so if provoked by largely unexpected political change? The gradual emergence within the political system of distinctive Islamicist parties is an important factor in this debate. The initiative began in the 1960s within the Center-Right Justice Party. Subsequent formulations came and went in the decades that follow (the name of the party changes constantly), leading bit by bit to electoral success. In 1995, the Welfare Party achieved some 20 per cent of the vote; this in turn led one year later to participation in government. The reaction, however, was swift: in 1998 both the Welfare Party and its leader Necmettin Erbakan were banned from politics for five years, on the grounds that they had participated in anti-secular activities. Despite such setbacks, another "religion-oriented" party, the AKP (Justice and Development Party), finally gained power in 2002. Both the Prime Minister (Recep Tayyip Erdogan) and the then Foreign Minister (Abdullah Gul) had an Islamicist background, indicating a significant shift in Turkey's political life. Just five years later, Abdullah Gul was elected President of the Republic, following a protracted and controversial election. The consequences of the 2007 election are still unclear.[3]

The gradual emergence of the religious factor as a central issue in Turkey's accession to the European Union reflects these changes. It is a debate which moves in stages. Initially—that is, in the early stage of the accession process—the insistence on secularism, both ideologically and in practice, was seen as a necessary step towards Europe; this was strongly supported by the military. Gradually however it became apparent that too strong an emphasis on secularism was running the risk of violating, rather than protecting, the place of the active Muslim constituency in the democratic process. The latter, moreover, were becoming increasingly aware that accession to the European Union was likely to enhance rather than impede their role in Turkish society. It is, therefore, the Islamicist AKP that in 2007 is edging Turkey towards membership of the European Union; conversely the military—one of the strongest advocates of secularism in Turkish society—are beginning to resist, appreciating that becoming part of Europe may for them be detrimental, limiting rather than supporting their position within the republic. Hence an unlikely logic: "Christian" Europe appears to be more generous to the Islamicists than "secular" Turkey (Fokas 2004, 2008).

That is one side of the story. The other can be found in Europe itself, for which the accession of Turkey to the European Union poses questions similar to those already raised concerning the place of religion in public as well as private life.[4] More profoundly, the negotiations surrounding this issue have become a trigger for an important but unresolved debate concerning the identity of Europe. Should this or should this not include a religious dimension? And if so, how should this be expressed? The questions are perplexing in themselves; so too the reasons for ignoring them for so long. Both are confronted in the essays brought together by Byrnes and Katzenstein (2006) who conclude somewhat pessimistically—religion is likely to become more rather than less problematic in southeastern Europe as the century progresses. Time will tell. In the meantime, the final irony concerning Turkey's position lies in the French case. The nation on which the Turkish constitution is modeled, becomes the nation most implacably opposed to Turkish entry. No one expressed this more forcibly than Giscard d'Estaing, the former French President and architect of the European Constitution. For Giscard, Turkey's capital is not in Europe and 95 per cent of its population live outside Europe; it is not therefore a European country. It follows that those who persist in backing Turkey's accession are quite simply "the adversaries of the European Union".[5]

As a footnote to this section, it is worth asking whether this discussion is simply one more instance of European unease about Islam or whether there are different issues at stake. The gradual accommodation of Orthodoxy within the European Union is interesting in this respect, in so far as it raises—yet again—the core identity of Europe. Is this rooted in Christianity as such or has it more to do with the legacies of Western Christendom? If the latter is the case, similar difficulties may arise as more Orthodox countries are considered for admission to the European Union, bearing in mind that Greece has been a member since 1981. So far the inclusion of Romania and Bulgaria has been relatively smooth. The case of Serbia however—inextricably linked to Russia and to Russian interests—is likely to be less straightforward. It would be unwise, to say the least, to ignore the religious dimension of this debate.

Working Towards a Conclusion: One West or Two?

Gathering up the threads of this chapter, it is clear that religion is becoming an ever more salient factor in both the United States and in Europe, but in different ways. In the former, religion continues to play a central, if at times disputed, role in civic as well as public life, not to mention its influence in foreign affairs. In the latter, the phrase "post-secular" is bit by bit asserting itself, albeit through clenched teeth. Each continent, moreover, continues to regard the other with a certain amount of suspicion—attitudes that are colored by very different assumptions about the rightful place of religion in national and international affairs. The ambiguities which emerge are best expressed in a series of questions, each of which evokes a particular facet of the problem. Four of these will be taken in turn in order to work towards a conclusion—not only to this chapter, but to the book as a whole. They are: is religion the wedge that will drive Europe away from the United States or is there a sufficient, indeed a growing, commonality between the two to maintain an effective alliance? What, secondly, is the place of Britain in these necessarily complex relations? To what extent, thirdly, is the debate influenced by a changing global context, within which religion is growing in importance almost by the day? And what, finally, should be the response of social science to these increasingly urgent questions?

One point has been made clear from the outset. The tensions between the United States and Europe are nothing new. No one denies that they have become both more vocal and more explicit under the Bush administration, but the roots go much deeper. Two very pertinent publications—Philippe Roger's *L'ennemi americain: Généalogie de l'antiaméricanisme français* (2002) and Jean-François Revel's *L'obsession anti-américaine: Son fonctionnement, ses causes, ses inconséquences* (2002)—offer an excellent illustration of these deep-seated antagonisms, using the French case as the primary example.[6] Their simultaneous appearance in 2002 is significant in itself. Equally important is the fact that both texts are essentially about France, not about America—neither author expects the American situation to change as a result of their writing, nor do they necessarily condone the French (indeed the European) position. Both, however, evoke a worldview which dominates political discourse in France, seeing this not so much as a reaction to the intricacies of American policy-making—whether in the Middle East or anywhere else—but as an entrenched resistance to a way of life which is inimical to French self-understanding. A second and very interesting theme follows from this: French hesitations about America derive as much from the political Right as they do from the political Left.

More precisely, thinkers on both sides of the political spectrum take exception to what they see as the "absolute capitalism" of the United States. The Left resists the extremes of the market for obvious and oft-repeated reasons, in which a strong state able to care for its people in a moral as well as practical sense plays a central role (see Variation Three). The hesitations of the Right draw on a very different tradition—nicely captured (particularly for Roger) in the work of Charles Maurras, the founder in the inter-war years of the controversial and barely democratic *Action Française*.[7] For Maurras, Catholic corporatism was evidently superior to American (Protestant) liberalism, which became in turn a threat to European—meaning Latin—civilization. So far so good: the logic of the argument is plain enough. Maurras's explicit, and increasingly unpleasant anti-Semitism is more difficult to accept. It supplied, however, a narrative in which America becomes the land of rootless immigrants including disproportionate numbers of (Germanophile) Jews. Hence an evident collusion between Right and Left, united—for different reasons—by a widespread distrust of a society that gave free rein to the market at the expense of more humane concerns.

A perceptive reviewer of both volumes (Mead 2003) asks an additional question. Setting the discussion into a global context, Mead introduces the links between French anti-Americanism and an even more deep-seated Anglophobia. Is the former, in other words, simply the latter writ large? Long-term economic as well as political humiliations have bred in the French a resentment of the Anglo-Saxon (both British and American) which is difficult to shift. The rifts over the war with Iraq are but the latest episode in a continually unfolding story.

The place of Britain in these subtle and complex equations has arisen in every one of our variations. In the first, it was far from clear where the real boundary lay in terms of religious cultures: is this to be found between the United States and Europe, or between Catholic Europe and the markedly different Protestant north, itself divided between the

Lutherans of Scandinavia and the more pluralist Anglo-Dutch cases? The analyses of France set out above quite plainly fall into the latter category, indicating clear blue water between French understandings on one side and Anglo-Saxon on the other. Such a view was strongly reinforced in our second variation with its emphasis on the different understandings of the Enlightenment. Himmelfarb (2004)—it will be remembered—strongly endorses an Anglo-Saxon alliance, seeing in the British Enlightenment the antecedents of the American case. Conversely, Himmelfarb is as questioning of the French case as the subjects of Roger's and Revel's analyses are of the American. To what extent this mutual and long-lasting incomprehension can be overcome by the innovative and energetic President Sarkozy remains to be seen.

The third variation underlined, above all, the institutional structures of Europe's historic churches. It is these, more than anything, that pull even Britain towards its continental neighbors. And if the power of these churches to discipline the beliefs and behavior of twenty-first-century Europeans is seriously diminished (no-one disputes this), their legacies remain—notably in a very different understanding of the state, itself responsible for the collective delivery of welfare so dear to Europeans. Religious mentalities, it is clear, are far more durable than religious organizations. It is for this reason that Europe, including Britain, cannot simply become American in terms of its religious life, however much a market in religious goods begins to emerge and however much English-speaking Evangelicals might like this. Even rational choice theorists must accept this limitation: vicarious religion, the residual public utility, will endure for the foreseeable future. What emerge in fact are two distinct sociologically explicable cases, one on each side of the Atlantic. It is unlikely that their paths will converge even if elements of one can be seen in the other. Nor is it necessary to decide which is right and which is wrong: they are simply different.

Both, however, are subject to change—not least in their relationships with the outside world. One manifestation of this relationship simply reinforces the contrasts already made (both above and in Variation Four). In America an already extensive religious diversity can expand to accommodate the newly arrived from wherever they come; in Europe the challenge to territory must always be taken into account. The latter, however, can no longer resist the mobilities of the modern world—a fact that is now beginning to disturb the Nordic and Mediterranean countries as much as it did the larger economies of western Europe for most of the post-war period. In the Mediterranean countries in particular, the flows reversed almost over night: societies of emigration turned imperceptibly into societies of immigration, which—unsurprisingly—were quite unprepared for the consequences. The Orthodox case is particularly problematic: autocephalous churches bolster national identities and vice versa. Hence, among other things, a continuing resistance to proselytism by faiths other than Orthodoxy.

Like it or not, this situation will persist: the outside world will continue to penetrate both the United States and Europe. Indeed in a global context, an approach which compares *only* the United States and Europe becomes increasingly inadequate. Precisely this point was raised at the end of Variation Two, in a discussion that introduced the notion of alternate or multiple modernities. Initially the focus lay on Europe as the distinctive case. If, however, the lens is widened further still—in order to look not only at Europe, but at "the West" as a whole from outside—the contours begin to alter. The differences between the two continents begin to diminish as an entirely new range of possibilities is taken into account. The latter include: the truly exponential growth of Christianity in the global south; the very different nature of the Muslim world (in all its manifest diversity); the emergence of new fault-lines which run through as well as between religions; and the noticeably different understandings of what it means to be modern in the Near, Middle, and Far East. All of these, moreover, are becoming increasingly visible almost by the day.

These are complex issues. And if it is difficult at times to deal with religion in the relatively mature democracies of the Western world (i.e., in both Europe and the United States), it is very much more so in a context where the political structures are markedly less stable. And whilst it is true that the arrival of new forms of religion in the West has on occasion challenged Western ways of doing things, the systems as such remain intact. Even more importantly, Western democracies share their core elements, not least the rule of law. A well-known commentator on European affairs, Timothy Garton Ash, grasps this nettle very firmly. Seen from outside— that is, from much of the developing world—the "hyperbolic claims of civilizational difference between 'old Europe' and the United States do not merely seem artificial; they seem criminally self-indulgent" (2004: 183). They can be categorized, following Sigmund Freud's contemptuous phrase, as the "narcissism of minor differences." The case of Britain, moreover, is central. Janus-faced Britain should become not a wedge, but a bridge to a better world—exploiting rather than bemoaning its multiple affinities. How to do this forms the substance of much of Garton Ash's current writing.

Rather more modestly, we would claim that religion is part and parcel of this process. Properly understood, it need not be the source of mutual hostility: it becomes instead one institution among many in the different configurations that make up the United States and Europe. Effective policy-making, moreover, will exploit this potential, optimizing the role of religion in either case—building on its more constructive elements and minimizing those that are likely to erode the common good. But in order that this should be so, religion must, surely, be taken into account in any informed analysis of trans-Atlantic relations, as indeed of the modern world taken as whole. How can this be ensured?

A Theoretical Postscript

Quite clearly, such an approach—together with the evidence on which it rests—is not much helped by the so-called secularization theory. It can, however (as already suggested) draw on innovative understandings of modernity.

To recapitulate: secularization theory was coined in the 1950s, though its core idea has much older antecedents. The idea can be simply stated: the historical development of recent centuries has brought about a progressive decline of religion, and there is every reason to believe that this decline will continue. It has by now become clear that this view of history was a grand extrapolation of the European experience, but it continues to be the starting point of many observers of the contemporary scene (though the majority of sociologists no longer share this assumption). There have been many reasons for the demise of secularization theory, notably the massive resurgence of religious movements in most of the world. But the America–Europe comparison is a big nail in the coffin of the theory: America is too big a society to fit comfortably under the maxim that the exception proves the rule. More importantly, though, the comparison impinges on a key proposition of secularization theory—namely, that it is modernity which brings about the decline of religion. It is difficult to argue that America is less modern than, say, Belgium. Minimally, this suggests that modernity can come in more than one version—and if this is the case with regard to religion, it is likely to be so with regard to other features of society.

Secularization theory was one component of a theory of modernity that could be described as a seamless-cloth view: modernity has certain defining features and (though not necessarily simultaneously) they make up a unified package—one feature follows another with something close to necessity. (Social scientists will recall here the influential works of Talcott Parsons and Marion Levy, though their ideas were anticipated in the classical works of Emile Durkheim and Max Weber.) One may caricaturize this view as the dropped-toothbrush theory of modernity: Drop an electric toothbrush into the Amazonian jungle, and a generation or so later the place will look like Cleveland (or, if you prefer, Düsseldorf). Like most social-scientific theories, there is a kernel of truth here: there are indeed some features of modernity that necessarily come in a package. Thus, if a society wishes to make use of certain forms of technology, it must accommodate its institutions and its cultural values so as to train people who can employ this technology. For example, a pilot of a modern aircraft cannot operate it on the metaphysical assumptions and the incantations of shamanic magic—*as long as he or she sits in the cockpit*. But when the pilot goes home—say, to an ancestral village—he or she can engage any number of magical ideas and practices.

It is precisely this idea that Shmuel Eisenstadt has developed in the notion of "multiple modernities." Modernity does indeed have some universally necessary features, notably those pertaining to science and technology, and when these are institutionalized they have certain likely social and cultural effects. Nevertheless, modernity comes in more than one version. A key case in point is that of Japan (which Eisenstadt discussed at length). Japan was the first non-Western nation to modernize successfully, beginning with the Meiji Restoration (more aptly called the Meiji Revolution) of 1868. But today Japan is as much a modern society as any in Europe or North America. Yet it has retained cultural, social, and even political features which are decidedly non-Western and which have their roots in centuries of Japanese tradition. But there are other cases: Soviet-style socialism, while it lasted, was also a case of an alternate modernity (as nicely expressed in the phrase "the Second World"), and its collapse was not due to its lack of modernity. What is more, in many countries of the developing world (previously known as "the Third World") there are powerful aspirations to modernize—but with this or that difference (differences, that is, from "the First World" of the West). These differences may be defined politically, socially, or culturally. Thus some thinkers in eastern Asia believe in modernity managed by authoritarian rather than democratic regimes (that notion also carries resonance in Russia), some in India want a modernity that can incorporate caste as a vital social institution, and some Africans want a modernity that will adjust to traditional cultural values of *ubuntu* (broadly understood as a distinctively African form of human solidarity). For the purpose of the present discussion it is irrelevant whether these ideas are intellectually coherent or whether they are likely to succeed. The point is that they are empirically present realities and their success cannot be ruled out a priori (vide Japan).

The concept of multiple modernities implies that Western modernity is not the only conceivable one and that modernity can come with this or that indigenous difference. This difference can also be in the matter of religion. It is precisely religion that defines the aspiration to an alternate modernity in many parts of the world today—a Russian modernity that will be inspired by the religious genius of Orthodoxy, an Islamic modernity (to paraphrase Lenin, *shari'a* with electrification), a Hindu modernity (*hindutva*), and for that matter an integrally Catholic modernity (Opus Dei has successfully practiced this one). The old secularization theory looked on all such aspirations as illusory. Social scientists have now become more cautious. These are interesting theoretical considerations in themselves (and one is free to say—may they never be of use to anyone). It so happens that they are useful, even politically useful. In many parts of the world the West is perceived pejoratively as propagating a culture of irreligious materialism. This perception is reinforced both by the influence of Western intellectuals (who are indeed heavily secular, even in the United States) and by the omnipresence of Western (mainly American) mass media, much of whose contents can rather accurately be described as irreligious and materialistic. The comparison between the United States and Europe provides an important counter-image, as does a more balanced view of European secularity. Put simply, here is an important example of how modernity can come in both secular and religious packages. This should be of some interest for the public diplomacy of Western democracies.

It should also be of use to scholars of society in the broadest sense of the term. Economic, political, and social scientists—whether interested in religion or not—should ponder carefully the implications of the previous paragraphs. What, in short, are the consequences of taking seriously the fact that for the great majority of the world's populations in the twenty-first century, it is not only possible, but entirely "normal," to be both fully modern and fully religious? Might this make a difference to the paradigms that we construct to understand better the nature of the modern world, whether European, American or more generally? The answer must surely be "yes." Indeed to follow this through would eliminate at a stroke what the British sociologist, James Beckford, has termed the insulation and isolation of the sociology of religion. Putting the same point more positively, it would once and for all restore religion to its rightful place in the social scientific agenda.

Notes

1 The provenance of this chapter requires a little explanation. A first draft (by Peter Berger) came at an early stage in the proceedings and pre-dated the variations. It was effectively the sequel to Chapter 2. As the variations evolved, however—each of them taking on a life of its own—it became clear that a number of the points originally raised in this chapter had already been covered. The text has been revisited in light of this, minimizing—if not entirely eradicating—the overlap in content.

2 See, for example, "God's Country? Evangelicals and U.S. Foreign Policy": http://pewresearch.org/pubs/73/gods-country (accessed 6 May 2008), a Pew Forum discussion following the publication of Walter Mead's *Foreign Affairs*

article entitled "God's Country?" (Mead 2006). See also: http://pewforum.org/press/?ReleaseID=33 (accessed 6 May 2008).

3   At the time of writing (Autumn 2007), there is considerable speculation about the next stage in Turkey's somewhat checkered democracy. The post of president brings with it considerable power, not least in terms of the army. Will the latter—a bastion of secularism and a crucial element in Turkish society—accept these changes, or will it intervene in the democratic process? The precedents regarding the latter are hardly reassuring.

4   For more on this subject, that is, on the Turkish case and beyond, see Fokas (2008, forthcoming).

5   These sentiments appeared in *Le Monde*. See BBC (2002) for an English version.

6   Both books have been translated into English: *The American Enemy: The History of French Anti-Americanism* (Roger 2006) and *Anti-Americanism* (Revel 2003).

7   The classic account in English of *Action Française* can be found in Weber (2005).

Bibliography

Adler, J. (2006). "The new naysayers. In the midst of religious revival, three scholars argue that atheism is smarter." *Newsweek* (11 Sept.).

Ahern G. and G. Davie. (1987). *Inner City God: The Nature of Belief in the Inner City* (London: Hodder and Stoughton).

Al-Azmeh, A. and E. Fokas (eds). (2007). *Islam in Europe: Diversity, Identity and Influence* (Cambridge: Cambridge University Press).

Albert-Llorca, M. (1996). "Rénouveau de la religion locale en Espagne." In G. Davie (ed.), *Identités religeuses en Europe* (Paris: La Découverte), pp. 235–52.

Ammerman, N. (1997). *Congregation and Community* (New Brunswick, NJ: Rutgers).

—— (2005). *Pillars of Faith: American Congregations and their Partners* (Berkeley, CA: University of California Press).

Banchoff, T. (ed.). (2007). *Democracy and the New Religious Pluralism* (New York: Oxford University Press).

Bastian, J.-P. and J.-F. Collange (eds). (1999). *L'Europe à la recherche de son âme* (Geneva: Labor et Fides).

Baubérot, J. (1990). *Vers un nouveau pacte laïque?* (Paris: Seuil).

—— (1997). *La morale laïque contre l'ordre moral* (Paris : Seuil).

—— (2005). *Histoire de la laïcité en France* (Paris: Presses Universitaires de France).

Bawer, B. (2006). *While Europe Slept* (New York: Doubleday).

BBC. (2002). "Turkey entry would 'destroy EU'." BBC News (8 Nov.); available online at http://news.bbc.co.uk/2/hi/europe/2420697.stm (accessed 6 May 2008)

Becker, G. (1976). *The Economic Approach to Human Behaviour* (Chicago: University of Chicago Press).

Becker, P. and H. Hofmeister. (2001). "Work, family, and religious involvement for men and women." *Journal for the Scientific Study of Religion* 40: 707–22.

Bellah, R. (1970). *Beyond Belief* (London: Harper and Row).

Berger, P. (ed.). (1999). *The Desecularization of the World: Resurgent Religion and World Politics* (Grand Rapids, MI: Eerdmans Publishing Co).

—— (2005). "Religion and the West." *The National Interest.* (Summer): 112–19.

Blaschke, O. (2000). "Das 19. Jahrhundert. Ein zweites konfessionelles Zeitalter?" *Geschichte und Gesellschaft* 26: 38–75.

—— (ed.). (2002). *Konfessionen im Konflikt. Deutschland zwischen 1800 und 1970: Ein zweites konfessionelles Zeitalter* (Göttingen: Vandenhoek & Ruprecht).

Boddie, S. and R. Cnaan. (2007). *Faith-Based Social Services: Measures, Assessments, and Effectiveness* (New York: Haworth Press).

Bordas, M. (2001). "Social welfare reform: Comparative perspectives on Europe and the United States." *International Journal of Public Administration* 24(2): 225–233.

Bouretz, P. (2000). "La democratie francaise au risque du monde." In M. Sadoun (ed.), *La democratie en France*: vol. 1, *Idéologies* (Paris: Gallimard), pp. 27–137.

—— (2001). "Secularity vs. laïcité: A comparative perspective" (unpublished paper, presented at the Berlin workshop, March).

Bréchon , P. (2001). "L'évolution du religieux." *Futuribles* 260: 39–48.

Brown, C. (2000). *The Death of Christian Britain* (London: Routledge).

Bruce, S. (1996). *Religion in the Modern World: From Cathedrals to Cults* (Oxford: Oxford University Press).

—— (2002). *God is Dead: Secularization in the West* (Oxford: Blackwell).

Buruma, I. (2006). *Murder in Amsterdam. The Death of Theo van Gogh and the Limits of Tolerance* (New York: Penguin).

Byrnes, T. and P. Katzenstein. (2006). *Religion in an Expanding Europe* (Cambridge: Cambridge University Press).

Casanova, J. (1994). *Public Religions in the Modern World* (Chicago: Chicago University Press).

—— (2003). "Beyond Europe and American exceptionalisms." In G. Davie, P. Heelas, and L. Woodhead (eds), *Predicting Religion: Christian, Secular and Alternative Futures* (Aldershot: Ashgate), pp. 17–29.

—— (2006). "Religion, European secular identities, and European integration." In T. Byrnes and P. Katzenstein (eds), *Religion in an Expanding Europe* (Cambridge: Cambridge University Press), pp. 65–92.

—— (2007). "Immigration and the new religious pluralism: A European Union/United States comparison." In T. Banchoff (ed.), *Democracy and the New Religious Pluralism* (New York: Oxford University Press), pp. 59–83.

Cesari, J. (2004). *Islam in the West* (Basingstoke: Palgrave MacMillan).

Cesari, J. and S. McLoughlin (eds). (2005). *European Muslims and the Secular State* (Aldershot: Ashgate).

Cnaan, R. (2002). *The Invisible Caring Hand: American Congregations and the Provision of Welfare* (New York: New York University Press).

Cnaan, R., S. Boddie, C. McGrew, and J. Kang. (2006). *The Other Philadelphia Story: How Local Congregations Support Quality of Life in Urban America* (Philadelphia: University of Philadelphia Press).

Cohen, A. and H. Koenig. (2003). "Religion, religiosity and spirituality in the biopsychosocial model of health and aging." *Ageing International* 28(3): 215–41.

Davie, G. (1994). *Religion in Britain since 1945: Believing without Belonging* (Oxford: Blackwell).

—— (2000). *Religion in Modern Europe: A Memory Mutates* (Oxford: Oxford University Press).

—— (2002). *Europe: The Exceptional Case: Parameters of Faith in the Modern World* (London: Darton, Longman and Todd).

—— (2005). "From obligation to consumption: A framework for reflection in Northern Europe." *Political Theology* 6(3): 281–301.

—— (2006a). "Is Europe an exceptional case?" *The Hedgehog Review* 8(1–2): 23–35.

—— (2006b). "Religion in Europe in the 21st century: The factors to take into account." *Archives européennes de sociologie/ European Journal of Sociology/ Europaeisches Archiv für Soziologie* XLVII(2): 271–96.

—— (2007a). "Vicarious religion: A methodological challenge." In N. Ammerman (ed.), *Everyday Religion: Observing Modern Religious Lives* (New York: Oxford University Press), pp. 21–36.

—— (2007b). *The Sociology of Religion* (London: Sage).

—— (2007c). "Pluralism, tolerance and democracy: Theory and practice in Europe." In T. Banchoff (ed.), *Democracy and the New Religious Pluralism* (New York: Oxford University Press), pp. 223–42.

Davie, G. and D. Martin. (1999). "Liturgy and music." In T. Walter (ed.), *The Week Diana Died.* (London: Berg), pp. 197–8.

Davie, G. and J. Vincent. (1998). "Progress report. Religion and old age." *Ageing and Society* 18(1): 101–10.

Davis, D. (2001). "Separation, integration, and accommodation: Religion and state in America in a nutshell." *Journal of Church and State* 43(1): 5–17.

—— (2003a). "Thoughts on the separation of church and state under the administration of President George W. Bush." *Journal of Church and State* 45(2): 229–35.

—— (2003b). "The Pledge of Allegiance and American values." *Journal of Church and State* 45(4): 657–68.

Dawkins, R. (2006). *The God Delusion* (London: Bantam Press).

Day, A. (2006). "Believing in belonging: A qualitative analysis of being Christian for the 2001 census." Paper presented to the 2006 Conference of the British Sociological Association Sociology of Religion Study Group, Manchester.

Dennett, D. (2006). *Breaking the Spell: Religion as a Natural Phenomenon* (New York: Viking).

De Vaus, D. (1984). "Workforce participation and sex differences in church attendance". *Review of Religious Research* 25(3): 247–56.

De Vaus, D. and I. McAllister. (1987). "Gender differences in religion." *American Sociological Review* 52(4): 472–81.

Dimitropoulos, P. (2001). *State and Church: A Difficult Relationship* (Athens: Kritiki) [in Greek].

Ebaugh, H. R. (2003). "Religion and the new immigrants." In Michele Dillon (ed.), *Handbook of the Sociology of Religion* (Cambridge: Cambridge University Press), pp. 225–39.

The Economist. (2005). "Welcome to the confused and the confusing world of European Islam." 377(8450) (29 Oct.): 87.

Eisenstadt, S. (2000). "Multiple modernities." *Daedalus* 129: 1–30.

Esping-Anderson, G. (1989). *The Three Worlds of Welfare Capitalism* (Cambridge: Polity Press).

Esposito, J., S. Nyang, and Z. Bukhari (eds). (2004). *Muslims' Place in the American Public Square: Hope, Fears, and Aspirations* (Lanham, MD: Rowman & Littlefield).

Fetzer, J. and J. C. Soper (2004). *Muslims and the State in Britain, France, and Germany* (Cambridge: Cambridge University Press).

Flannelly, K., A. Weaver, D. Larson, and H. Koenig (2002). "A review of mortality research on clergy and other religious professionals." *Journal of Religion and Health* 41(1): 57–68.

Fokas, E. (2004). "Turkey, Islam and the European Union." In N. Canefe and M. Ugur (eds), *Turkey and European Integration: Accession Prospects and Issues* (London: Routledge Press), pp. 147–70.

—— (2008). "Islam in the framework of Turkey-EU relations: Situations in flux and moving targets." *Global Change, Peace and Security* 20(1): 87–98.

—— (forthcoming). "Religion: towards a post-secular Europe?" In C. Rumford (ed.), *Sage Handbook of European Studies* (London: Sage).

Francis. L. (1997). "The psychology of gender differences in religion: A review of empirical research." *Religion* 27(1): 81–96.

—— (2003). "Religion and social capital." In P. Avis (ed.), *Public Faith: The State of Religious Belief and Practice in Britain* (London: SPCK), pp. 45–64.

Fulton, J., T. Dowling, A. Abela, I. Borowik, P. Marler, and L. Tomasi. (2000). Y*oung Catholics at the New Millennium: The Religion and Morality of Young Adults in Western Countries* (Dublin: University College Dublin Press).

Garton Ash, T. (2004). *Free World: Why a Crisis of the West Reveals the Opportunity of our Time* (London: Allen Lane).

Gauchet, M. (1985). *Le désenchantement du monde: une histoire politique de la religion* (Paris: Gallimard).

—— (1999). *The Disenchantment of the World* (Leiden: Brill).

Geaves, R., T. Gabriel, and Y. Haddad (2004). *Islam and the West Post-September 11th* (Aldershot: Ashgate).

Gomez-Quintero, A. (2004). "Religious education in the Spanish school system." *Journal of Church and State* 46(3): 561–73.

Gunn, J. (2004). "Under God but not the scarf: The founding myths of religious freedom in the United States and laïcité in France." *Journal of Church and State* 46(1): 7–24.

Habermas, J. (2005). "Religion in the public sphere" (lecture presented at the Holberg Prize Seminar, 29 Nov.); available online at: http://www.holbergprisen.no/downloads/diverse/hp/hp_2005/2005_hp_jurgenhabermas_religioninthepublicsphere.pdf (accessed 6 May 2008).

—— (2006). "Religion in the public sphere." *European Journal of Philosophy* 14(1): 1–25.

Habermas, J. and J. Ratzinger. (2006). *The Dialectics of Secularization: On Reason and Religion* (San Francisco: Ignatius Press).

Hadaway, K., P. Marler, and M. Chaves. (1993). "What the polls don't show: a closer look at church attendance." *American Sociological Review* 58(6): 741–52.

—— (1998). "A symposium on church attendance." *American Sociological Review* 63(1): 111–45.

Haddad, Y. and J. Smith (eds). (1993). *Mission to America: Five Islamic Sectarian Movements in North America* (Gainesville, FL: University of Florida Press).

Harris, S. (2006). *The End of Faith: Religion, Terror, and the Future of Reason* (London: Free Press).

—— (2007). *Letter to a Christian Nation* (London: Bantam Press).

Henry, P. (1981). " 'And I don't care what it is': The tradition-history of a civil religion proof-text." *Journal of the American Academy of Religion* 49(1): 35–49.

Herberg, W. (1965). *Protestant—Catholic—Jew* (New York: Doubleday).

Hervieu-Léger, D. (2000). *Religion as a Chain of Memory* (Cambridge: Polity Press) [translation of *La religion pour mémoire*, 1993].

—— (2001a). *La Religion en miettes ou la question des sectes* (Paris: Calmann-Lévy).

—— (2001b). "France's obsession with the 'sectarian threat'." *Nova Religio* 4: 249–58.

—— (2003). *Catholicisme, la fin d'un monde* (Paris: Bayard).

Higgens, A. (2007). "The new crusaders: As religious strife goes, Europe's atheists seize pulpit." *The Wall Street Journal* (12 April): A1.

Himmelfarb, G. (2004). *The Roads to Modernity: The British, French and American Enlightenments* (New York: Vintage Books).

Hitchens, C. (2007). *God is Not Great: The Case Against Religion* (London: Atlantic Books).

Howard, C. (1993). "The hidden side of the American welfare state." *Political Science Quarterly* 108(3): 403–436.

Hunter, J. (1991). *Culture Wars: The Struggle to Define America* (New York: Basic Books).

Huntington, S. (1998). *The Clash of Civilizations and the Remaking of World Order* (New York: Simon and Schuster).

Jackson, R. (2004). *Rethinking Religious Education and Plurality: Issues in Diversity and Pedagogy* (London: RoutledgeFalmer).

—— (2007). "European institutions and the contribution of studies of religious diversity to education for democratic citizenship." In R. Jackson, S. Miedema, W. Weisse, and J-P. Willaime (eds), *Religion, Diversity and Education in Europe* (Münster: Waxmann Verlag), pp. 22–56.

Jenkins, P. (2002). *The Next Christendom: The Coming of Global Christianity* (New York: Oxford University Press).

—— (2007). *God's Continent: Christianity, Islam, and Europe's Religious Crisis* (New York: Oxford University Press).

Johnson, G. (2000). "British social democracy and religion, 1881–1911." *Journal of Ecclesiastical History* 51(1): 94–115.

Klausen, J. (2005). *The Islamic Challenge: Politics and Religion in Western Europe* (Oxford: Oxford University Press).

Knauth, T. (2007). "Religious education in Germany: Contribution to dialogue or source of conflict?" In R. Jackson, S. Miedema, W. Weisse, and J-P. Willaime (eds), *Religion and Education in Europe: Developments, Contexts and Debates* (Münster: Waxmann Verlag), pp. 243–66.

Koenig, H., D. Larson, and D. Matthews. (1996). "Religion and psychotherapy with older adults." *Journal of Geriatric Psychiatry* 29(2): 155–94.

Lambert, Y. (2002). "Religion: l'Europe à un tournant." *Futuribles* 277: 129–60.

Levin, J. (ed.). (1994). *Religion in Aging and Health: Theoretical Foundations and Methodological Frontiers* (Thousand Oaks, CA: Sage).

Lewis, B. (1997). *The Future of the Middle East* (London: Orion).

—— (2003). *The Crisis of Islam: Holy War and Unholy Terror* (New York: The Modern Library).

Livezey, L. (ed.). (2000). *Public Religion and Urban Transformation: Faith in the City* (New York: New York University Press).

Lyon, D. and M. Van Die. (2000). *Rethinking Church, State and Modernity: Canada between Europe and the USA* (Toronto: Univeristy of Toronto Press).

Madeley, J. (2003). "European liberal democracy and the principle of state religious neutrality." *Western European Politics* 26(1): 1–22.

Madeley, J. and Z. Enyedi. (2003). *Church and State in Contemporary Europe: The Chimera of Neutrality* (London: Frank Cass).

Manion, M. (2002). "Churches and states: The politics of accommodation." *Journal of Church and State* 44(2): 317–43.

Martin, B. (2000). "The Pentecostal gender paradox: A cautionary tale for the sociology of religion." In R. Fenn (ed.), *The Blackwell Companion to the Sociology of Religion* (Oxford: Blackwell), pp. 52–66.

—— (2003). "Beyond measurement: The non-quantifiable religious dimension in social life". In P. Avis (ed.), *Public Faith: The State of Religious Belief and Practice in Britain* (London: SPCK), pp. 1–18.

Martin, D. (1978). *A General Theory of Secularization* (Oxford: Blackwell).

—— (1996). *Reflections on Sociology and Theology* (Oxford: Clarendon Press).

—— (2005). *On Secularization: Towards a Revised General Theory* (Aldershot: Ashgate).

Mazzotti, M. (2001). "Maria Gaetana Agnesi: Mathematics and the making of Catholic enlightenment." *Isis* 92(4): 657–83.

—— (2007). *The World of Maria Gaetana Agnesi, Mathematician of God* (Baltimore, MA: Johns Hopkins University Press).

McLeod, H. (2000). *Secularisation in Western Europe, 1848–1914* (Basingstoke: Palgrave Macmillan).

Mead, W.R. (2003). "Why do they hate us? Two books take aim at French anti-Americanism." *Foreign Affairs* (March/April): 139–42.

—— (2006). "God's Country?" *Foreign Affairs* (September/October): 24–44.

Messbarger, R. and P. Fidlen. (2005). *The Contest for Knowledge: Debates Over Women's Learning in Eighteenth-Century Italy (The Other Voice in Early Modern Europe)* (Chicago: University of Chicago Press).

Miller, A. and R. Stark. (2002). "Gender and religiousness: Can socialization explanations be saved?" *American Journal of Sociology* 107(6): 1399–423.

Monsma, S. (2000). "Substantive neutrality as a basis for free exercise–no establishment common ground." *Journal of Church and State* 42(1): 13–35.

Muller, S. (1997). "Time to kill: Europe and the politics of leisure." *The National Interest* 48: 26–36.

Nielsen, J. (2004) [1992]. *Muslims in Western Europe* (Edinburgh: University of Edinburgh Press).

Norris, P. and R. Inglehart. (2004). *Sacred and Secular. Religion and Politics Worldwide* (Cambridge: Cambridge University Press).

Pepper, S. (1982). "The conundrum of the free exercise clause: Some reflections on recent cases." *Northern Kentucky Law Review* 9: 265–303.

Pierson, G.W. (1938). *Tocqueville and Beaumont in America* (New York: Oxford University Press).

Poulat, E. (1987). *Liberté-Laïcité. La guerre des deux France and le principe de la modernité.* (Paris: Cerf/Cujas).

Raedts, P. (2004). "The church as nation state: A new look at ultramontanist Catholicism." Paper presented at conference on Alternate Master Narratives of Religion in the Modern World, University of Amsterdam.

Ratzinger, J. and M. Pera. (2006). *Without Roots: Europe, Relativism, Christianity and Islam* (New York: Basic Books).

Revel, J.-F. (2002). *L'obsession anti-américaine: Son fonctionnement, ses causes, ses inconséquences* (Paris: Plon).

—— (2003). *Anti-Americanism* (New York: Encounter Books).

Robbers, G. (ed.). (2005). *State and Church in the European Union* (Baden-Baden : Nomos Verlagsgesellschaft).

Roberts-DeGennaro, M. (2006). "Executive orders for the faith-based and community initiatives." *Journal of Policy Practice* 5(4): 55–68.

Roger, P. (2002). *L'ennemi americain: Généalogie de l'antiaméricanisme français* (Paris: Seuil).

—— (2006). *The American Enemy: The History of French Anti-Americanism* (Chicago: University of Chicago Press).

Savage, S., S. Collins-Mayo, B. Mayo, and G. Cray. (2006). *Making Sense of Generation Y: The World View of 15- to 25-Year-Olds* (London: Church House Publishing).

Schlesinger, P. and F. Foret. (2006). "Political roof and sacred canopy? Religion and the EU constitution." *European Journal of Social Theory* 9(1): 59–81.

Shapiro, R. and J. Young. (1989). "Public opinion and the welfare state: The United States in comparative perspective." *Political Science Quarterly* 104(1): 59–89.

Simmons, P. (2000). "Religious liberty and abortion policy: Casey as 'catch-22'." *Journal of Church and State* 42(1): 69–88.

Skeie, G. (2007). "Religion and education in Norway." In R. Jackson, S. Miedema, W. Weisse, and J.-P. Willaime (eds), *Religion and Education in Europe: Developments, Contexts and Debates* (Münster: Waxmann Verlag), pp. 221–42.

Smith, C. (1998). *American Evangelicalism: Embattled and Thriving* (Chicago: Chicago University Press).

—— (2000). *Christian America? What Evangelicals Really Want* (Berkeley, CA: University of California Press).

—— (2005). *Soul Searching: The Religious and Spiritual Lives of American Teenagers* (New York: Oxford University Press).

Smith, C., M. Emerson, S. Gallagher, P. Kennedy, and D. Sikkink. (1998). *American Evangelicalism: Embattled and Thriving* (Chicago: University of Chicago Press).

Smith, J. (1999). *Islam in America* (New York: Columbia University Press).

Stark, R. (2002). "Physiology and faith: Addressing the 'universal' gender difference in religious commitment." *Journal for the Scientific Study of Religion* 41(3): 495–507.

Ter Avest, I., C. Bakker, G. Bertram-Troost, and S. Miedema. (2007). "Religion and education in the Dutch pillarized and post-pillarized educational system." In R. Jackson, S. Miedema, W. Weisse, and J.-P. Willaime (eds), *Religion and Education in Europe: Developments, Contexts and Debates* (Münster: Waxmann Verlag), pp. 203–219.

Uddin, Baroness Pola Manzila. (2002). "Multi-ethnicity and multi-culturalism." House of Lords Hansard (20 Mar.): 1423.

Van Kersbergen, K. and P. Manow. (forthcoming). *Religion, Class Coalitions and Welfare State Regimes* (Cambridge: Cambridge University Press).

Voas, D. (2003a). "Is Britain a Christian country?" In P. Avis (ed.), *Public Faith? The State of Religious Belief and Practice in Britain* (London: SPCK), pp. 92–105.

—— (2003b). "Intermarriage and the demography of secularisation." *British Journal of Sociology* 54(1): 83–108.

Voas, D. and S. Bruce. (2004). "Research note: The 2001 census and Christian identification in Britain." *Journal of Contemporary Religion* 19(1): 23–8.

Wallis, J. (2005). *God's Politics: Why the Right Gets It Wrong and the Left Doesn't Get It* (New York: HarperOne).

Walter, A. and G. Davie. (1998). "The religiosity of women in the modern West." *British Journal of Sociology* 49(4): 640–60.

Warner, S. (1993). "Work in progress towards a new paradigm for the sociological study of religion in the United States." *American Journal of Sociology* 98(3): 1044–93.

—— (1997). "A paradigm is not a theory: Reply to Lechner." *American Journal of Sociology* 103(1): 192–8.

Weber, E. (2005). *Action Francaise: Royalism and Reaction in Twentieth-century France* (Palo Alto, CA: Stanford University Press).

Weigel, G. (2006). *The Cube and the Cathedral: Europe, America and Politics without God* (New York: Basic Books).

Weller, P. (2004) "Identity politics and the future(s) of religion in the UK: The case of the religion questions in the 2001 decennial census." *Journal of Contemporary Religion* 19(1): 3–21.

Wilcox, C. and T. Jelen. (2002). "Religion and politics in an open market: Religious mobilization in the United States." In T. Jelen and C. Wilcox (eds), *Religion and Politics in Comparative Perspective: The One, the Few and the Many* (Cambridge: Cambridge University Press), pp. 289–313.

Willaime, J.-P. (2007). "Different models for religion and education in Europe." In R. Jackson, S. Miedema, W. Weisse, and J.-P. Willaime (eds), *Religion, Diversity and Education in Europe* (Münster: Waxmann Verlag), pp. 57–66.

Wilson, B. (1969). *Religion in Secular Society: A Sociological Comment* (Harmondsworth: Penguin).

—— (1982). *Religion in Sociological Perspective* (Oxford: Oxford University Press).

—— (1998). "The secularization thesis: Criticisms and rebuttals." In B. Wilson, J. Billiet, and R. Laermans (eds), *Secularization and Social Integration: Papers in Honour of Karel Dobbelaere* (Leuven: Leuven University Press), pp. 45–66.

Woodhead, L. (2000). "Women and religion." In L. Woodhead, P. Fletcher, H. Kawanami, and D. Smith (eds), *Religions in the Modern World* (London: Routledge), pp. 332–56.

—— (2002) "Feminism and the sociology of religion: From gender-blindness to gendered difference." In R. Fenn (ed.), *The Blackwell Companion to the Sociology of Religion* (Oxford: Blackwell), pp. 67–84.

Woolever, C., D. Bruce, K. Wulff, and I. Smith-Williams. (2006). "The gender ratio in the pews: Consequences for religious vitality." *Journal of Beliefs and Values* 27(1): 25–38.

Young, L. (ed.). (1997). *Rational Choice Theory and Religion* (New York: Routledge).

Websites

http://www.bu.edu/cura/about/introduction.html
http://www.student.teol.uu.se/tres/
http://www.statistics.gov.uk/census2001/census2001.asp
http://hirr.hartsem.edu/research/research_congregtnl_studies.html
http://pewforum.org/events/index.php
http://eurel.u-strasbg.fr/EN/index.php
http://www.whitehouse.gov/government/fbci/president-initiative.html
http://www.theocracywatch.org/faith_base.htm
http://www.europeanvalues.nl/
http://www.youthandreligion.org/research/
http://www.firstamendmentcenter.org/news.aspx?id=12755
http://pewresearch.org/pubs/73/gods-country
http://pewforum.org/press/?ReleaseID=33

Index